Architectural History after Colvin

The Society of Architectural Historians of Great Britain

Symposium, 2011

edited by Malcolm Airs and William Whyte

T.S. LA FONTAINE.
MAR '81

ARCHITECTURAL HISTORY AFTER COLVIN

THE SOCIETY OF ARCHITECTURAL HISTORIANS OF GREAT BRITAIN SYMPOSIUM, 2011

edited by

MALCOLM AIRS

and

WILLIAM WHYTE

SHAUN TYAS
DONINGTON
2013

Typeset from the discs of the editors and designed by the publisher

Published by

SHAUN TYAS
1 High Street
Donington
Lincolnshire
PE11 4TA

ISBN
978-1-907730-32-0

The editors and publisher are pleased to acknowledge with thanks the financial support of the Society of Architectural Historians of Great Britain and from the President and Fellows of St John's College, Oxford, which made this publication possible.

Printed and bound in Great Britain by Butler Tanner and Dennis, Frome

Contents

Preface

This book is a memorial to one of Britain's most distinguished scholars. But it is also the memento of an enormously enjoyable summer's day at St John's College, Oxford, where more than a hundred architectural historians gathered to pay tribute to Sir Howard Colvin and to consider the future direction of our discipline. It was an event which concluded with the unveiling of a plaque in Canterbury Quad, the subject of one of Colvin's numerous books and the focus of an essay in the present volume. We have deliberately sought to retain the relaxed and informal atmosphere of the day. The chapters which follow are – in the main – re-workings of the talks that were given at the symposium.

We are grateful to our contributors for their hard work, and to those in the audience who offered such helpful advice and criticism. We must also thank the scholars who chaired the symposium: Richard Hewlings, Frank Kelsall, Elizabeth McKellar, and Geoffrey Tyack; the volunteers who helped run the event: Philip Aspin, Oliver Cox, and Alex Echlin; and Kathryn Morrison, chairman of the SAHGB, for her tremendous support. *Architectural History After Colvin* would have been inconceivable without the financial contributions of both the Society of Architectural Historians of Great Britain and – especially – St John's College. The logistical and intellectual help given by Sam Brewitt-Taylor was also crucial and we are extremely thankful that he was willing to become an honorary architectural historian for the occasion.

Malcolm Airs
William Whyte

List of Contributors

Malcolm Airs is an historian who has been actively involved with the conservation movement since starting work with the Greater London Council in 1966. He was conservation officer in South Oxfordshire from 1974 to 1991 before taking up a post at Oxford University Department for Continuing Education to develop a programme in architectural history and historic conservation. He has recently retired as Director of the Centre for the Historic Environment at Kellogg College. He is a past President of the Institute for Historic Building Conservation and is currently President of the Society of Architectural Historians of Great Britain. His DPhil thesis was examined by Howard Colvin and he subsequently served with him on a number of local and national committees.

LIST OF CONTRIBUTORS

As pupil, co-author and colleague, **Joe Mordaunt Crook** worked with Howard Colvin for half a century. He has been Public Orator and Professor of Architectural History at London University, as well as Slade Professor and Waynflete Lecturer at Oxford where he is now an Honorary Fellow of Brasenose. He is the author of many works, including *The British Museum* (1971), *The Greek Revival* (1972), *William Burges* (1981; second edition, 2013), *The Dilemma of Style* (1987), *The Rise of the Nouveaux Riches* (1999), *The Architect's Secret* (2003) and *Brasenose: the biography of an Oxford college* (2008).

Anthony Geraghty is Senior Lecturer in the History of Art at the University of York. His catalogue of the Wren drawings at All Souls College, Oxford was published by Lund Humphries in 2007. He has just published a book called *The Sheldonian Theatre: architecture and learning in early-modern England*. Howard Colvin informally co-supervised his PhD dissertation in the mid-1990s.

John Harris was formerly Curator of the British Architectural Library's Drawings Collection and has been 55 years in the Trade.

Alan Powers was until recently Professor of Architecture and Cultural History at the University of Greenwich. He wrote his PhD at Cambridge under the supervision of Sir John Summerson and has subsequently worked as a writer, exhibition curator, and conservationist, not least as Chairman of the Twentieth Century Society. Recent books include *Britain* in the series Modern Architectures in History (2007), *Aldington Craig and Collinge* (2009), and *Robin Hood Gardens Re-Visions* (Twentieth Century Society, 2010).

Andrew Saint has been Editor of the *Survey of London*, the official history of London's buildings, since 2006. He has written a number of books including *Richard Norman Shaw* (1976, second edition 2010), *The Image of the Architect* (1983), *Towards A Social Architecture: the role of England in post-war school-building* (1987), and *Architect and Engineer: a study in sibling rivalry* (2007). Between 1995 and 2006 he was a professor in the Department of Architecture at Cambridge. He writes: 'I first met Howard Colvin in about 1969, when writing my first scholarly article, 'Three Oxford Architects', which was partly about the Victorian development of the St John's estate in North Oxford under William Wilkinson. Howard was friendly and helpful, allowing me to see some of the St John's records which were relevant, but he made it quietly clear that he thought the buildings I was interested in were pretty horrid.'

Frank Salmon is Senior Lecturer in the History of Art at the University of Cambridge, and a Fellow and Tutor of St John's College, Cambridge. Prior to that he worked at the Paul Mellon Centre for Studies in British Art and the University of Manchester. His most recent book is the edited volume *The Persistence of the Classical: essays on architecture presented to David Watkin* (2008). He is currently working on the English Italianate revival of the nineteenth century.

Simon Thurley studied at Bedford College and the Courtauld Institute before becoming an Assistant Inspector at English Heritage and then Curator of the Historic Royal Palaces. In 1998 he became Director of the Museum of London and in 2003 Chief Executive of English Heritage. His books include monographs on Whitehall Palace, Hampton Court and Somerset House. He is currently writing a one-volume history of English architecture for Harper Collins. Simon is Honorary Fellow at Royal Holloway College and Visiting Professor of the Built Environment at Gresham College.

William Whyte is fellow and tutor in history at St John's College, Oxford. He is the author of *Oxford Jackson: architecture, education, status, and style, 1835–1924* (2006) which was based on a thesis co-supervised by Joe Mordaunt Crook, and has since co-edited several other books. He is currently completing *Redbrick: a Social and Architectural History of Britain's Civic Universities* for publication in 2014.

List of Figures

Chapter One

THE SUCCESS OF SIR HOWARD COLVIN AND THE CURIOUS FAILURE OF ARCHITECTURAL HISTORY

William Whyte

Sir Howard Colvin's death in December 2007 was widely recognized as marking the end of an era.[1] Hailed as 'the greatest architectural historian of his own time, and perhaps ever', he was seen as one of the heroes of the heroic age of architectural history.[2] 'It is difficult now to appreciate how generally amateur and backward architectural history was', observed another obituarist; 'it was Colvin's achievement to place British architectural history on a sound scholarly basis'.[3] Nor were these encomia unprecedented. Nearly fifty years before, in an article on architectural historians which profiled John Summerson, Dorothy Stroud, Christopher Hussey, and Margaret Whinney as well as Howard Colvin, it was the latter who was identified as 'pretty well the most knowledgeable architectural historian in the country'.[4] Small wonder that when David Watkin published his own history of architectural history in 1980 he described something called the 'Colvin revolution': an approach which 'changed the face of English architectural history.'[5]

The decision to a hold a symposium in memory of Howard Colvin can consequently be defended purely because of the importance his work alone. That he, in the words of Anthony Geraghty, 'played a central role in the development of architectural history in Great Britain' now goes without saying.[6] But our intention was to do more than just commemorate the life of a significant scholar.[7] To examine the 'Colvin revolution' is to beg questions about the very nature of the subject he helped to define. Was architectural history before Colvin actually mired in the sorts of dilettantism and 'irresponsible attributionism' that he would later decry?[8] Was his own approach really as original as his admirers later

1 For their comments on early versions of this chapter, I am hugely grateful to Malcolm Airs, Joe Mordaunt Crook, Anthony Geraghty, Dan Hicks, Elizabeth McKellar, and Zoë Waxman.

2 Richard Hewlings, 'Sir Howard Colvin', *Independent* 1 January 2008, p. 34.

3 'Sir Howard Colvin', *Daily Telegraph*, 7 January 2008, p. 27.

4 'Britain's Bricks and Mortar', *Home and Garden,* April 1960, pp. 70–73, p. 73.

5 David Watkin, *The Rise of Architectural History* (London, 1980), p. 161.

6 Anthony Geraghty, 'Howard Colvin', *Burlington Magazine* 150 (September 2008), pp. 613–14, p. 613.

7 William Whyte, 'Colvin: a commemoration', *SAHGB Newsletter* 103 (Summer 2011), pp. 1–3.

8 Howard Colvin, *Essays in Architectural History* (New Haven and London, 1999), pp. 292,

suggested; or, as critics have claimed, did the work of Colvin's generation actually amount to little more than the resurgence of antiquarianism?[9] Still more intriguingly, the symposium offered the opportunity to ask a question of more than merely historiographical interest: what should be the future of architectural history? Now that the 'Colvin revolution' is itself receding into the distant past, it is surely time for architectural historians to consider how the discipline should develop in the years to come.

The chapters which follow touch on each of these themes. They are all, in a sense, celebrations of Colvin's life and work; tributes to his commanding importance for the study of architectural history in Great Britain. Here Frank Salmon praises his imaginative reconstruction of unbuilt projects. Simon Thurley explores Colvin's pioneering efforts in establishing the history of *The King's Works*. Malcolm Airs draws attention to his unsung labours to secure the conservation of historic buildings. But none of our authors is uncritical. They point to gaps, blind spots, and opportunities not taken, and go on to suggest that the subject should now develop in very different ways. Andrew Saint, for example, argues that Colvin's *Dictionary* helped contribute to a narrowing of architectural history: an exclusive – and unhealthy – focus on the biography of individual architects. Anthony Geraghty re-examines Colvin's *Canterbury Quadrangle*, and concludes that it is 'a disappointing book' because it takes such a narrow view of architectural history. Alan Powers likewise remarks on the fact that Colvin's oeuvre took little account of the development of modern architecture and rested firmly on a purely empiricist approach, something that left it unable to speak to the current concerns of architects themselves.

In acknowledging both the strengths and the weaknesses of Howard Colvin's writing, this volume, we hope, pays proper tribute to a man who prized accuracy above everything. The same is true of the new directions in architectural history that our authors contemplate. As the author of a transformatively important book – the *Dictionary of British Architects;* as the editor of a massive, multi-volume, standard work – *The History of the King's Works*; as the writer, in his retirement, of a study which traced the development of a building type from classical antiquity onwards: Howard Colvin was nothing if not ambitious. It thus seems entirely appropriate that our authors have been similarly bold in their statements about the future of the subject. 'We are now free', Joe Mordaunt Crook concludes; 'free to do different things.'

294.

[9] Mark Swenarton, 'The Role of History in Architectural Education', *Architectural History* 30 (1987), pp. 201–15, p. 212.

It is in the same spirit that this introduction seeks to place Howard Colvin's career within a rather fuller historiographical perspective: examining the whole range of his writings – from important books to ostensibly insignificant book reviews, from architectural to administrative history; and seeking to explain the development of his thought in the broadest possible sense. As both Geraghty and Crook observe in their contributions, it is impossible to understand Colvin's significance without exploring the origins of his approach and the assumptions which underlay it. He himself claimed that he had done little more than 'to apply to architecture the ordinary processes of historical scholarship'.[10] But this, of course, is a statement that conceals as much as it reveals – not least because it raises the question of exactly what 'the ordinary processes of historical scholarship' amount to. More importantly still, it should compel architectural historians to query whether these processes are actually appropriate for the study of the built environment. Over the next few pages I shall argue that Colvin's success was based precisely on his ability to apply the historical methodology in which he had been trained to a new and different field of research. I will also, however, suggest that the adoption of practices and assumptions developed by conventional, textual historians proved, in the longer term, to be problematic.

* * *

In his youth, Howard Colvin dreamt of becoming an archaeologist. As a student, he was trained to be a medieval administrative historian. He made his name as an academic by writing on the architecture of early-modern England.[11] To reduce a long and distinguished career to such a short set of bald statements is, of course, to ignore a whole series of complexities – and to disregard the continuities that underlie ostensibly erratic development. As Simon Thurley shows in his chapter, for example, the research for *The King's Works* in reality involved much archaeology as well as medieval administrative history. Nonetheless, the story of Howard Colvin's intellectual and professional evolution is an intriguing one and sheds much light on the approach he was to take to architectural history. His assumptions about archaeology and administrative history and about the ways in which both could contribute to – and were different from – the study of architecture helped to define his work. Moreover, by highlighting these themes, it is possible to explore the ways in which this work related to wider developments in the writing of history, noting Colvin's very real originality as well as the similarities he shared with his contemporaries.

10 Colvin, *Essays in Architectural History*, p. 292.

11 J. Mordaunt Crook, 'Howard Montagu Colvin, 1919–2007', *Proceedings of the British Academy* CLXVI (Oxford, 2010); William Whyte, 'Colvin, Sir Howard Montagu (1919–2007)', *Oxford Dictionary of National Biography*.

Colvin's interest in archaeology was profound and precocious. At school in Derbyshire, he led a series of archaeological digs in nearby Dale Abbey, publishing his first article on the results aged only nineteen.[12] It was Sir Mortimer Wheeler, the pre-eminent archaeologist of the age, no less, who advised the adolescent Colvin to study history in preparation for a career in archaeology, not least – presumably – because there were almost no jobs in the field.[13] Even twenty years later in the late-1950s, indeed, only three universities in England would offer degrees in archaeology.[14] As an undergraduate at University College London, however, Colvin was able to take Wheeler's special subject on Anglo-Saxon archaeology and to participate in the excavations at Clarendon Palace which had been begun by the professor of art history Tancred Borenius. His wartime service, as an aerial photography analyst for the RAF, also depended in part on Colvin's archaeological interests. It is noteworthy, in particular, that the man who oversaw his training was Glyn Daniel, who in many ways succeeded Wheeler as the predominant figure in post-war British archaeology.[15] Nearly forty years later, he doubtless drew on youthful lessons at UCL in reviewing books like H. M. Taylor's encyclopaedic history of *Anglo-Saxon Architecture*.

In light of his own intellectual development, this short review of Taylor bears further examination. For one thing, it is striking – especially given Geraghty's critique in this volume – to see that amongst Colvin's own criticisms of Taylor was his lack of attention to context. 'The history of architecture', his review concluded, 'is rarely of much value if it is written without reference to the society that produced it.' Still more significantly, in making this claim, Colvin explicitly distinguished between 'archaeological and architectural history', on the one hand, and the 'institutional history' of the Church, on the other.[16] This was an important distinction, and one with a biographical as well as historiographical basis. For Colvin, of course, was himself by training an institutional historian of the Church. His well-received first book on the Premonstratensian order which had occupied Dale Abbey – *The White Canons in England* – was purely concerned with administrative history. Entirely typically, it corrected hundreds of errors in previous accounts,[17] and was 'completed by an almost impeccable

[12] H. M. Colvin, 'Excavations at Dale Abbey: interim report', *Derbyshire Archaeological and Natural History Society Journal* 12 (1938), pp. 87–94.

[13] H. M. Colvin, 'Early Life of Howard Colvin', unpublished MS.

[14] Christopher Gerrard, 'The Society for Medieval Archaeology: the early years (1956–62), in Roberta Gilchrist and Andrew Roberts, eds., *Reflections: 50 years of medieval archaeology, 1957–2007* (London, 2009), pp. 23–43, p. 30.

[15] Colvin, 'Early Life of Howard Colvin'.

[16] *English Historical Review* 94 (1979), pp. 114–16.

[17] Joseph A. Gribbin, *The Premonstratensian Order in Late-Medieval England* (Woodbridge, 2001), p. xvii.

index.'[18] But it took no interest in the religious views of the priests it studied and had nothing to say about the architecture or archaeology that had obviously sparked Colvin's interest in the order.[19] Here, then, was the complete reverse of Taylor's book: a volume only concerned with 'institutional history' to the total exclusion of 'archaeological and architectural history'.

The approach Howard Colvin took in his *White Canons* was to some extent dictated by circumstances. On demobilisation, he was offered a post as lecturer in medieval history at UCL by the head of department, J. E. Neale. Years later, Colvin recalled that one of the conditions of his appointment was that he registered for a doctorate. 'As it seemed unlikely that anything architectural would find favour with Neale (who was a ruthless sacker of those who lost his favour)', he wrote, 'I decided to pursue my schoolboy interest in the Premonstratensians.'[20] It is certainly true that it was Colvin's election to a fellowship at St John's College, Oxford in 1947 that enabled what he later described as 'a double life as a medievalist and an architectural historian'.[21] Freed from the demands of Neale's 'absolute monarchy' at UCL,[22] he discovered 'that Oxford was a place where, once established, one could do whatever one liked provided only that one did not neglect one's pupils'.[23] Without this freedom, and compelled to satisfy Neale, it is scarcely surprising that his first book should ignore the architectural and archaeological in favour of the institutional.

Yet there were also more positive – and more important – reasons why Colvin's first book took the form it did. As a student he had not just concentrated on archaeological options. He had fallen under the influence of the young and newly-appointed medievalist John Le Patourel, who shared his interest in architecture and possessed a similarly photographic memory, and who published his own first book, *The Medieval Administration of the Channel Islands*, in the year Colvin arrived at the college.[24] He also took the optional subject set up by H. A. Cronne on medieval ecclesiastical institutions and, when UCL was evacuated to Aberystwyth, he was impressed by the medieval constitutional historian Reginald Treharne. Above all, Colvin was taken up by V. H. Galbraith, director of the Institute of Historical Research from 1944 to 1948, when he

18 Marjorie Chibnall in *English Historical Review* 99 (1954), pp. 91–94, p.93.
19 H. M. Colvin, *The White Canons in England* (Oxford, 1951), p. 1.
20 H. M. Colvin to Nigel Ramsay (24 April 2004), unpublished letter.
21 Quoted in Jeremy Musson, 'Sir Howard Colvin: leading architectural historian', *Country Life*, 3 May 2007, p. 120
22 N. B. Harte, *One Hundred and Fifty Years of History Teaching at University College London* (London, 1982, p. 21.
23 Colvin, 'Early Life of Howard Colvin'.
24 J. C. Holt, 'John Le Patourel', *Proceedings of the British Academy* LXXI (Oxford, 1986).

became Regius Professor at Oxford. It was Galbraith who supervised the research for the *White Canons*, Galbraith who persuaded Oxford University Press to publish the book, and Galbraith who arranged for Howard Colvin to be appointed to a fellowship at St John's.[25]

The training Colvin received as undergraduate, with its emphasis on the mastery of archival material and the importance of administrative structures, perfectly prepared him for the writing of institutional history. Moreover, as Joe Mordaunt Crook observes in his chapter, all his medieval history tutors were, in one way or another, the products of a similar tradition: an approach that developed in Oxford under William Stubbs and had been transplanted to Manchester under T. F. Tout and Maurice Powicke. 'If Tout was Stubbs's pupil, Powicke was Tout's: and I am theirs', observed Galbraith in his Oxford inaugural lecture.[26] The same was true for Le Patourel, who was also taught by Powicke, and for Treharne, who had studied at Manchester. It was even true for Harry Cronne, who was inducted into 'the research methods of the Manchester School' as an undergraduate at Queen's University of Belfast.[27] It was from this tradition that Colvin developed his own sense of what the 'ordinary processes of historical scholarship' actually amounted to. Here was a scientific history of the sort exemplified in the accuracy and paleographic precision of *The White Canons in England*. As Galbraith put it, 'Clio, once a muse, is now more commonly seen, with a reader's ticket, verifying her references at the Public Record Office.'[28]

To embrace this approach was to join the elite of the historical profession: experts, not antiquaries; disinterested specialists rather than the *parti pris*. Constitutional history was to become the preserve of historians instead of lawyers or politicians. 'Ecclesiastical history likewise had become too important to leave to deans, bishops, and Dissenting ministers', in the words of Michael Bentley.[29] Tellingly, Galbraith praised the *White Canons* in precisely these terms. 'It is a relief', he wrote to OUP, 'to have someone working on the Middle Ages in an *objective* way – as an historian – with no theological axe to grind'.[30] And as if this were not enticing enough for an ambitious young historian in the 1940s, then the way in which this historiographical tradition was developing suggested that the

25 Colvin, 'Early Life of Howard Colvin'.

26 V. H. Galbraith, *Historical Study and the State* (Oxford, 1948), p. 4.

27 H. A. Cronne, T. W. Moody, and D. B. Quinn, eds., *Essays in British and Irish History in Honour of James Eadie Todd* (London, 1949), p. x.

28 V. H. Galbraith, *An Introduction to the Study of History* (London, 1964), p. 4.

29 Michael Bentley, 'Shape and Pattern in British Historical Writing, 1815–1945', in Stuart Macinty, Juan Maiguascha, and Attila Pók, eds., *The Oxford History of Historical Writing, vol. iv: 1800–1945* (Oxford, 2011), pp. 204–24, p. 221.

30 OUP Archives, PB/ED/006473, Galbraith to Dan Davin (2 December 1949).

future was an exciting one. Dissatisfied with the exclusive emphasis on purely constitutional history which they had inherited from Stubbs, Colvin's generation helped to expand the range of permissible subjects to study. They remained loyal to the Manchester school and to Galbraith – that 'fundamentalist apostle of documents'.[31] But they began to look further afield. Amongst Colvin's colleagues in Oxford, Richard Southern examined medieval intellectual history,[32] Marjorie Reeves explored the world of medieval millenarianism,[33] and Beryl Smalley reconstructed the mental world of medieval churchmen.[34] In writing about church administration in the middle ages, Colvin was thus at the cutting edge of the subject.[35] His patron Galbraith is again worth quoting, for it was he who identified Colvin as 'probably the best young medievalist since Dick Southern'.[36]

Even as Galbraith wrote, of course, he had to acknowledge that his protégé was unlikely to remain a medievalist. 'Colvin's interests extend to the 18 [*sic.*] century', he observed, 'and he will probably end up as the great authority on English architects!'[37] Nevertheless, the attitudes that Colvin imbibed as a young academic stayed with him. Not only, as Joe Mordaunt Crook notes, did he remain attracted to the study of institutions; Colvin also continued to follow many of his mentors' dictums about the nature of historical research itself. His 'strategy' in compiling the *Dictionary* was twofold: 'to concentrate on exploiting all the major sources of architectural writing in turn' and 'to identify as far as possible the authorship of certain categories of important buildings'.[38] By using archival research to further a prosopographical project in this way, Colvin was thus remaining true to his early training whilst also contributing to the broadening of the Manchester school's approach. Similar impulses underwrote the work of Colvin's contemporary, K. B. McFarlane, in his researches on 'Bastard feudalism', which used a similar mastery of manuscript sources to build up patterns of patronage amongst the late-medieval aristocracy and gentry.[39]

[31] Alexander Murray, 'Richard William Southern, 1912–2001', *Proceedings of the British Academy* 120 (Oxford, 2003), pp. 413–44, p. 421.

[32] R. W. Southern, *The Shape and Substance of Academic History* (Oxford, 1961).

[33] R. W. Southern, 'Marjorie Reeves as a Historian', in R. J. Bartlett, ed., *History and Historians: selected papers of R. W. Southern* (Oxford, 2008), pp. 218–24.

[34] R. W. Southern, 'Beryl Smalley, 1905–1984', *Proceedings of the British Academy* 72 (1986), pp. 455–71.

[35] M. D. Knowles, 'Some Trends in Scholarship, 1868–1968, in the Field of Medieval History', *Transactions of the Royal Historical Society* 19 (1969), pp. 139–58, pp. 146–7.

[36] OUP Archives, PB/ED/006473, Galbraith to Dan Davin (2 December 1949).

[37] Ibid.

[38] Colvin, *Essays in Architectural History*, p. 295.

[39] Lawrence Stone, 'Prosopography', in idem., *The Past and Present Revisited* (London and New York, 1987), pp. 45–73, p. 55.

Indeed, viewed as part of a generation of scholars, Colvin's change of focus seems less remarkable – and less like a break from his initial formation as a historian. It is noteworthy, for example, that his rival for the St John's job – the formidable future fellow of Trinity College, Oxford, J. P. Cooper – read the whole of Tout's six volume *Chapters in the Administrative History of Medieval England* when still at school. Influenced by McFarlane, Cooper fully intended to become a medievalist himself, but instead transferred his interest to the economic history of the sixteenth and seventeenth centuries, becoming an expert on the archives of the great landed estates of that era.[40]

Lawrence Stone, Colvin's contemporary at nearby Wadham, pursued an even more circuitous route. His first book was, extraordinarily enough, a history of *Sculpture in Britain: the Middle Ages*. But he then went on to make a career anatomizing the early-modern period, drawing on immense archival research to produce huge – and hugely controversial – synthetic works.[41] Stone, in both style and substance, differed greatly from Colvin; yet in their move from the medieval to the early modern, in their commitment to 'scientific' history and the amassing of manuscript material, they shared a similar trajectory and some surprisingly similar assumptions.[42] They even co-authored a paper on the Howard tombs at Framlingham.[43]

It is little wonder that the early-modern period appealed to both men, for it was an alluring field for an enterprising historian in the mid-twentieth century.[44] Its archival deposits were rich and often untapped.[45] It was an era that seemed ripe for redefinition; indeed the very term 'early-modern' was a neologism, first coined in the 1930s and still controversial in the 1960s.[46] Above all, for many of Colvin's contemporaries the seventeenth century appeared to be, as the Tudor historian Geoffrey Elton put it, 'the crucial and transforming age in the history of English society.'[47] It attracted Marxists like Christopher Hill, Colvin's neighbour

40 G. E. Aylmer, 'J. P. Cooper as a Scholar', in G. E. Aylmer and J. S. Morrill, eds., *Land, Men, and Beliefs: studies in early-modern history* (London, 1983), pp. ix–xiii.

41 A. L. Beier, David Cannadine, and J. M. Rosenheim, eds., *The First Modern Society: essays in English history in honour of Lawrence Stone* (Cambridge, 1989).

42 David Cannadine, 'Historians in the "liberal hour": Lawrence Stone and J. H. Plumb re-visited', *Historical Research*, 75 (2002), pp. 316–54.

43 H. M. Colvin and Lawrence Stone, 'The Howard Tombs at Framlingham, Suffolk', *Archaeological Journal* 122 (1965), pp. 159–71.

44 See also Barbara Arciszewska, 'Classicism: constructing the paradigm in continental Europe and Britain', in Barbara Arciszewska and Elizabeth McKellar, eds., *Articulating British Classicism: new approaches to eighteenth-century Architecture* (Aldershot, 2004), pp. 1–34, p. 16.

45 Colvin, *Essays in Architectural History*, p. 295.

46 J. H. Elliott, *History in the Making* (New Haven and London, 2012), pp. 58–9.

47 G. R. Elton, *Modern Historians on British History, 1485–1945* (London, 1970), p. 51.

at Balliol College until his retirement in 1978,[48] and anti-Marxists like Hugh Trevor-Roper, Colvin's colleague within the Oxford history faculty until his retirement in 1980.[49] As Anthony Geraghty has shown, the sense that the seventeenth century marked a watershed in the cultural life of the country also influenced John Summerson, who adopted T. S. Eliot's schema, seeing it as the birth of the modern age.[50] In moving from the medieval to the early modern, Howard Colvin was part of the avant garde within his profession.

Although less typical of a discipline which continued to privilege the textual over the visual, this transition from purely institutional history to the study of more material themes was nonetheless also mirrored by others.[51] It is worth remarking, for example, that the only other historian at Oxford who wrote on similar subjects – the idiosyncratic fellow of Oriel, W. A. Pantin – announced his own change of focus at the time that Howard Colvin arrived in the university. Before the Second World War, Billy Pantin served as University Lecturer in Ecclesiastical Institutions; after it, he became lecturer in Medieval Archaeology and History. 'One of the disciples of Sir Maurice Powicke', and a former lecturer at Manchester, he too was part of the process whereby the Manchester school – the approach that Colvin himself embodied – came to broaden both its chronological and analytical range.[52]

If Colvin's intellectual evolution was neither as discontinuous nor as atypical as it may appear at first sight, then it nonetheless had a dramatic effect on the subject he now chose to study. It is true, as Anthony Geraghty observes in his chapter, that architectural history was not quite the slough of amateurism that Colvin's admirers later alleged. The work of the *Survey of London*, in particular, was meticulous and exacting enough even for him.[53] The discipline in Britain had, however, been overwhelmingly dominated by architects rather than historians.[54] Some, like the late-Victorian T. G. Jackson, had become significant authorities on

[48] See Tim Harris, 'Talking with Christopher Hill: part 1', in Geoff Eley and William Hunt, *Reviving the English Revolution: reflections and elaborations on the work of Christopher Hill* (London, 1988), pp. 99–103, pp. 99–100.

[49] See Peter Ghosh, 'Hugh Trevor-Roper and the History of Ideas', *History of European Ideas* 37 (2011), pp. 485–505, p. 503.

[50] Anthony Geraghty, 'The "dissociation of sensibility" and the "tyranny of intellect": T. S. Eliot, John Summerson, and Christopher Wren', in Frank Salmon, ed., *The Persistence of the Classical: essays on architecture presented to David Watkin* (London, 2008), pp. 26–39, pp. 28–9.

[51] Robert Tittler, *Architecture and Power: the town hall and the English urban community, c. 1500–1640* (Oxford, 1991), p. 1.

[52] M. D. Knowles, 'William Abel Pantin, 1902–1973', *Proceedings of the British Academy* 60 (1974), pp. 447–58, p. 457.

[53] H. M. Colvin, 'Architectural History and Its Records', *Archives* 2 (1954), pp. 300–11, p. 305.

[54] Watkin, *Rise of Architectural History*, cc. 3–4.

the archival sources for the subject.[55] Others, like his pupil Sir Charles Peers, had engaged in serious archaeological work.[56] But none had been trained in the research methods that Colvin had mastered; and few were capable of exploiting the range of resources that he now deployed. The rise of the Manchester school had not only opened new vistas, it had literally opened new archives – and Colvin was quick to use them too. The change was little less than the sort of paradigm shift anatomized by Thomas Kuhn a few years later, not least because Colvin's emphasis on documents solved questions of attribution which had long puzzled experts.[57] The *Dictionary* was consequently greeted as 'the authority we have all been wanting for years.'[58] Just as in many scientific revolutions, the 'Colvin revolution' saw an outsider apply methods developed in another, unrelated field with a transformative effect.[59] The fact that, at the same time, other scholars were embracing art-historical methods pioneered in Germany only made Colvin's achievement the more complete. Even they had to bow to his expertise. The enormously influential art historian Rudolf Wittkower found himself compelled to enquire, 'Do you know that young man at Oxford who has written this Dictionary of English Architects? I'll have to rethink my book on Lord Burlington.'[60]

This triumph was made all the more overwhelming by changes in the world of architecture. As Colvin wrote, the importance of history to the architectural profession – and to architectural training – was dwindling.[61] The modernists who came to dominate schools of architecture in the 1940s and 1950s abandoned the search for historical precedent to justify their work.[62] In Reyner Banham's words, despite 'a garland of references to Wittkower, Palladio, and the modulor', the new Brutalists, in particular, 'turned consciously to the great form givers of their time for inspiration', looking to Frank Lloyd Wright, Mies van der Rohe, and – above all – Le Corbusier instead.[63] Architectural history, and, as Alan Powers shows in this volume, especially the history of architecture before the twentieth century,

[55] William Whyte, *Oxford Jackson: architecture education, status, and style, 1835–1924* (Oxford, 2006), ch. 1.

[56] Nicholas Doggett, 'Peers, Sir Charles Reed (1868–1952)', *Oxford Dictionary of National Biography*.

[57] See, for example, [Laurence Whistler], *Times Literary Supplement*, 5 November 1954.

[58] *Sunday Times*, 12 September 1954.

[59] Thomas Kuhn, *The Structure of Scientific Revolutions* (Chicago, 1962).

[60] Quoted in John Harris, *Apollo* 1995, p. 68.

[61] Neil Jackson, 'Where Now the Architect?', *Transactions of the Royal Historical Society* 13 (2003), pp. 207–17; Watkin, *Rise of Architectural History*, pp. 145–59.

[62] On the triumph of the modernists, see John R. Gold, *The Practice of Modernism: modern architects and urban transformation, 1954–1972* (London and New York, 2007), pp. 27–30.

[63] Reyner Banham, *The New Brutalism: ethic or aesthetic?* (London, 1966), p. 15.

was consequently at a discount: 'demoted from the role of the great teacher of form'.[64] The architectural profession increasingly withdrew from historical research, leaving the field free for historians; and many historians – not least John Summerson after 1957 – similarly stopped writing architectural criticism.[65] Nikolaus Pevsner, whose work continued to combine historical research with the aggressive promotion of the International Modern style, found himself 'out of date' by the 1960s;[66] 'an authority' whom ambitious architects 'had to reject'.[67] This environment created new opportunities for historians like Colvin, with his lack of public involvement in contemporary architecture an index of his seriousness as a scholar. His refusal to study architectural form for its own sake was also legitimated by these developments. Just as architects – and those who taught them – came to reject the 'genealogies of form' that accounted for even the most assertively contemporary buildings by analogy to historic precedent;[68] so architectural historians like Wittkower came to abandon formalist analysis as dangerously subjective.[69] Colvin's archival researches, in this context, seemed attractively objective by comparison.

Given Howard Colvin's personal predilections – he was, recalled Keith Thomas, 'a firm empiricist, not a speculative thinker, and he lacked any interest in theory or in large-scale interpretations of historical change';[70] given his training as a historian; and given the monumental success of his work: it is scarcely a surprise that his underlying assumptions about the practice of history changed little over the years. The scope of his researches widened and the sources he consulted became still more various. But the method was the same – and the results continued to be more than well received. The publication of the *Dictionary*'s second edition was greeted by Hugh Honour as 'an event which calls for a triumphal arch'.[71] The completion of the *King's Works* was likewise, asserted Geoffrey Elton, 'an occasion which calls for trumpets.'[72] As new archival sources continued to be found or acquired by records offices,[73] and as Colvin

64 Reyner Banham, 'Historical Studies and Architectural Criticism', *Transactions of the Bartlett Society* 1962–3, pp. 3–52, p. 5.

65 Elizabeth McKeller, 'Popularism versus Professionalism: John Summerson and the twentieth-century creation of the "Georgian"', in Arciszewska and McKeller, eds., *Articulating British Classicism*, pp. 35–56, p. 42.

66 Susie Harris, *Nikolaus Pevsner: the life* (London, 2011), ch. 36.

67 Banham, *New Brutalism*, p. 14.

68 Banham, 'Historical Studies', p. 38.

69 Alina A. Payne, 'Rudolf Wittkower and Architectural Principles in the Age of Modernism', *Journal of the Society of Architectural Historians* 53 (1998), pp. 322–42, p. 325.

70 Keith Thomas, in *Sir Howard Montague* [sic.] *Colvin, 1919–2007* (Oxford, 2008), p. 8.

71 Hugh Honour, *Observer*, 16 April 1978.

72 G. R. Elton, *English Historical Review* 99 (1984), pp. 106–108, p. 206.

73 For example: Iain Gordon Brown in *Journal of the Society of Archivists* 17 (1996), pp. 223–4.

received corrections and clarifications from around the world, there can have seemed little need to change a winning formula.[74]

Indeed, Howard Colvin's commitment to this particular notion of historical research evidently intensified rather than diminished after the publication of the *Dictionary*. This was a development signalled by his growing unwillingness to be seen as archaeologist. In 1957, as he joined Billy Pantin, W. G. Hoskins, and other Oxford colleagues in helping to found the Society for Medieval Archaeology, he expressed worries about how 'orthodox' historians would react to this activity. One solution was to appoint Pantin as the first president; but even then Colvin appears to have been unhappy at his association with an explicitly archaeological group. In 1958, he wrote offering to resign, and although he saw out his term of office as a council member, he never again came to any meetings.[75] At the same time, Colvin began explicitly to identify himself as a 'documentary historian': a term that occurs repeatedly in his book reviews from the early-1960s onwards. Although, in 1964, he did refer to the 'present *rapprochement* between documentary historians and archaeologists', it is clear on which side of the divide he was positioning himself.[76] Intriguingly, he even used this professional identity to plead ignorance of architecture. Reviewing B. G. Morgan's *Canonic Design in Medieval Architecture*, for example, Colvin observed that 'On his architectural conclusions it is less easy for a documentary historian to comment.'[77] Such a conscious self-fashioning perhaps helps to explain why Colvin was not one of the leading figures in the foundation of the Society of Architectural Historians of Great Britain. Although he was persuaded to sit on the editorial board of *Architectural History*, he was not on the founding council. Strikingly, when the SAHGB came to Oxford in 1960, it was Pantin, rather than Colvin, who lectured – 'with indomitable zest' – on domestic architecture in the city.[78] x

It is hard not to conclude that Colvin's identification as a 'documentary historian' was strategic. As he admitted in 1954, architectural history was not just a 'marginal subject', but a 'historical Cinderella'.[79] More than twenty years later, he was forced to accept that it was still 'marginal', though now 'well enough established in its own peripheral territory'.[80] An emphasis on the importance of archival exactitude appears to have been synonymous in his own mind with what

[74] See, Colvin, 'Writing *A Biographical Dictionary of British Architects*', in his *Essays on Architectural History*, pp. 292–7.
[75] Gerrard, 'The Society for Medieval Archaeology: the early years', pp. 32, 36.
[76] *English Historical Review* 79 (1964), p. 140.
[77] *English Historical Review* 78 (1963), pp. 762–4, p. 763.
[78] *Architectural History* 4 (1961), p. 93.
[79] Colvin, 'Architectural History and Its Records', p. 300.
[80] H. M. Colvin, *English Architectural History: a guide to sources* (London, 1976), p. 1.

x In 1960 I was not a member of SAH nor did I become one until 1970s.

he called 'the present age of professional historiography';[81] 'the academic approach to architectural history which [had] developed since the Second World War.'[82] In other words, by emphasising documentary research above all else – even to the apparent exclusion of his own interest in archaeology – Colvin sought to establish the *bona fides* of his own discipline. It was an effort rewarded with no small success. As Keith Thomas recalled, 'By applying the techniques familiar in the study of medieval history, he rendered architectural history academically respectable.'[83]

With hindsight, however, it is possible to see that such success came at a cost. For one thing, as Mark Swenarton complained in the late-1980s, documentary history of the sort practised by Colvin and his followers had almost nothing to say to those members of the architectural profession who wanted to take history more seriously; for them it was pure 'antiquarianism', with no relevance to current questions about design.[84] Worse still, even those who sought to remedy this situation ended up unwittingly reinstating a division between (practical) architect and (factual) historian. 'There is a need for historians who will provide the objective facts', observed Derek Linstrum in 1987. 'But there is also a need for architect/historians who know how designs evolve, how structures and materials behave'.[85] That architectural historians might need to think about both was something Colvin had noted thirty years before.[86] Yet such was the force of the conceptual distinction that he himself had helped to shape, it has proved all too enduring.[87]

Historiographically, too, there were losses as well as gains from this approach. Colvin's heroic labours in the archives yielded rich results: an unrivalled accuracy in attribution in his *Dictionary*; a magisterial command of administrative history in the *King's Works*; a wholly new way of seeing the evolution of university architecture in *Unbuilt Oxford*. But his approach to research was not unproblematic. Mining documents for facts necessarily meant treating them primarily as sources of data than as subjects of interest in their own right. A case in point is his treatment of John Aubrey's 'Chronologia Architectonica', which, as Olivia Horsfall-Turner has recently noted, Colvin saw

81 *English Historical Review* 94 (1979), p. 436.
82 *English Historical Review* 98 (1982), p. 837.
83 Thomas in *Howard Montague* [sic] *Colvin*, p. 4.
84 Swenarton, 'Role of the Architect', p. 212.
85 Derek Linstrum, 'The Uses of Architectural History Today', in Ben Farmer and Henty Louw, eds, *A Companion to Contemporary Architectural Thought* (London, 1993), pp. 227–30, p. 230.
86 Colvin, 'Architectural History and Its Records', p. 300.
87 See also Joan Kerr, 'Why Architects Should Not Write Architectural History', in Andrew Leach, Antony Moulis, and Nicole Sully, eds., *Shifting Views: selected essays on the architectural history of Australia and New Zealand* (St Lucia, 2008), pp. 23–31.

as pioneering but ultimately flawed: 'In light of the fact that Aubrey's schema was not entirely accurate ... he concluded that its major value was that it provided visual evidence of a number of buildings that no longer exist.'[88] Yet, as Horsfall-Turner goes on to show, such a conclusion was an impoverished one, ignoring the real importance of Aubrey's work in helping to define the nature of architectural history in general and wholly missing its significance in explaining early-modern attitudes to the Gothic in particular.

As Michael Bentley has shown, this was typical of the Manchester school – or, as he terms them, the 'Modernists' – who had trained Colvin. For them,

> The task of writing history ... had an investigative aspect aimed at 'the sources': one began with 'research' in order to acquire 'the facts' and having retrieved or 'discovered' them, the project involved writing a text that gave a fair, accurate and balanced account of what had been found.[89]

The problem, as Bentley goes on to argue, was that these assumptions were easily confused; so that historians conflated 'facts' with 'the evidence' and 'the evidence' with 'the sources' themselves, ignoring the real distinction between 'sources' (the surviving remains of a period) and 'evidence' (a subset of sources used to make a historical argument).

> Method in this respect turned into a hunt for 'new material', unearthing that unseen letter or an unnoticed section of a charter, and the subject thus became 'source-led', rather than following a range of questions or hypothesis.[90]

This was an invitation to ever-narrower research, 'with documentary verification for every proposition and documentary contextualization for each description.'[91]

It was also an approach which was being overturned in academic history. R. W. Southern's 1961 inaugural lecture, for example, was an attack on the constitutional and administrative history in which he had been trained – and it was just one of many contemporary assaults.[92] As a member of Southern's audience recalled, 'By the end, we knew that he had sounded the death-knell of the Pipe Roll.'[93] Yet, of course, Colvin's work never acknowledged any such

88 Olivia Horsfall-Turner, '"The Windows of this Church are of several Fashions": architectural form and historical method in John Aubrey's "Chronologia Architectonica"', *Architectural History* 54 (2011), pp. 171–93, p. 172.

89 Michael Bentley, *Modernizing England's Past: English historiography in the age of modernism, 1870–1970* (Cambridge, 2005), p. 9.

90 Ibid., p. 199.

91 Ibid., p. 207.

92 Southern, *Shape and Substance of Academic History*.

93 Peter Brown, quoted in Murray, 'Southern', p. 433.

thing. The Pipe Roll series was the first item in his 1964 essay on 'Architectural History and Its Records',[94] and remained so in its 1976 revision.[95] More importantly, the assumptions that underpinned his work were unshaken by the changes in practice that shook much of the rest of the historical profession from the 1960s onwards. The methods and themes of the Manchester school were overturned by new questions and new methodologies. The impact of the social sciences and, later, of the linguistic turn; the rise in awareness about the problems of the search for 'facts': all these helped challenge the assumptions that had driven his work. In a striking repudiation of his own career, Colvin's erstwhile collaborator Lawrence Stone was moved in 1979 to announce the death of 'scientific history' and the surprising 'revival of narrative'. No longer in search of facts, he argued, the historian now sought to evoke *mentalités*; no longer a scientist, the historian was now once again a storyteller.[96] This was a challenge to everything that Colvin stood for – but one that he did not address.

Fashions change in history. It would be wrong to berate Howard Colvin for not predicting – much less for not responding to – the critiques that arose decades after he first started writing. But the methodological weaknesses of the Manchester school were significant – and became ever-more apparent as his career went on. Moreover, his methods produced another, more general, problem for the development of architectural history in Britain. The price of what Keith Thomas termed academic respectability was what Colvin recognized as academic marginality. If architectural history was nothing more than documentary history applied to buildings, then it was destined to remain a 'Cinderella' subject. This was less to do with what one of Colvin's admirers called the 'inherited philistinism' of the historical establishment than it was to do with the fact that an architectural history which placed a primacy on textual evidence could scarcely be seen as the source of new knowledge or new approaches by other sorts of historians.[97] The dating of a building; the proper attribution of a detail; the discovery of new documents: these might all be interesting, but they would necessarily remain peripheral to most other scholars. Colvin made no claims that architectural history had a distinctive approach of its own, nor did he suggest that its methodologies could be applied to other fields; quite the reverse, as we have already noted, he always insisted he was doing nothing more than 'applying the ordinary processes of historical scholarship' to architecture. Yet in the absence of

94 'Colvin, Architectural History and Its Records', p. 306.

95 Colvin, *English Architectural History*, p. 5.

96 Lawrence Stone, 'The Revival of Narrative: reflections on an old new history', *Past and Present* 85 (1979), pp. 3–24.

97 R. A. Beddard, *English Historical Review* 96 (1981), pp. 872–7, p. 872.

a distinctive – and distinctively different – way of doing architectural history, it was unlikely that other historians would turn to specialists on architecture for anything more than illustrative material. A problem when the Manchester model was in the ascendant, this was a fatal flaw when 'scientific' history of the sort that Colvin had mastered fell out of favour.

As a consequence, Colvin's legacy was hugely impressive, but also somewhat ambiguous.[98] On the one hand, he left behind a strikingly important set of achievements: scores of articles; dozens of reviews; six volumes of the standard history of a government department; four editions of a fundamental work of reference; as well as editing other texts, contributing to public bodies, and supervising the graduate studies of leading figures in the next generation of historians. To read the *Festschrift* presented to him in 1984 is a daunting experience, for it reveals a man who really had helped to transform his subject.[99] To realise that he still had another two decades of research to go – years in which he published two revisions of the *Dictionary*, his books on *Canterbury Quadrangle*, *All Souls and Its Buildings*, *Calke Abbey*, and *Architecture and the After-Life*, as well as more than twenty other essays and edited texts – is to be staggered by his achievements. His approach to the subject continues to be influential, not least in the pages of periodicals like *Architectural History* and, especially, the *Georgian Group Journal*, where – as Andrew Saint notes in his chapter – the search for accurate attributions based on the serious study of archival material still goes on.

Colvin's wider impact, however, was more mixed. Institutionally, he left architectural history no stronger. It is an index of the subject's failure that his own post as Reader in Architectural History at Oxford was extinguished on his retirement. As a discipline, in Elizabeth McKellar's words, it remains the 'invisible subject': as marginal to departments of architecture, art history, and history, as ever before.[100] The current decline in heritage funding suggests that it may become weaker still, as conservation bodies and local authorities lose their trained architectural historians too.[101] The triumph of 'theory' over 'history' in architectural schools means that the gap between architects and architectural historians has grown no smaller. Even in the United States, where there was once optimism that the study of the past was becoming more important in the training

98 See also Dana Arnold, *Reading Architectural History* (London and New York, 2002), p. 41.

99 *Design and Practice in British Architecture: studies in architectural history presented to Howard Colvin* (*Architectural History* 27 [1984]).

100 Elizabeth McKellar, 'Architectural History: the invisible subject', *Journal of Architecture* 1 (1996), pp. 159–64.

101 Malcolm Airs, 'Architectural History in a Cold Climate', *SAHGB Newsletter* 102 (Winter/Spring 2011), pp. 1–3.

of future architects,[102] recent writings suggest growing doubt about the subject's viability without a greater capacity to convince practitioners of its relevance.[103] This institutional failure is surely linked to a deeper, more important, intellectual failure: the failure of architectural historians to create what McKellar terms, 'a credible and distinctive area of academic enquiry'; a field of study with its own logic, methods, and lessons to teach other subjects.[104] It is a failure for which Colvin was not, of course, wholly to blame. But it is one in which he was undeniably complicit.

***

Howard Colvin's achievements were immense and unrepeatable. His brilliant mind and remarkable capacity for hard work did indeed transform the discipline. My own admiration for him – and debt to him – has already been publicly stated and remains undiminished.[105] Nonetheless, as this book shows and as my introduction has, I hope, further demonstrated, the world after Colvin is a very different place. If it is to survive, architectural history needs to reach out to precisely those places and people that Colvin's approach could not and did not touch. It needs to re-engage with the architectural profession and to persuade other historians that it has something to teach them too. Above all, it needs a clarity about its subject matter and about the distinctiveness of its methodology that it currently lacks.[106] To reach that goal we may need to supersede much of the work that Howard Colvin did, we may even need to reject many of his assumptions. But the great lesson of Colvin's career is surely just this: that it is indeed possible to reshape a subject. We need only to be as bold – and as unsentimental – as Howard himself once was.

102 Stanford Anderson, 'Architectural History in Schools of Architecture', *Journal of the Society of Architectural Historians* 58 (1999), pp. 282–90.

103 Nancy Stieber, 'Architectural History Between Disciplines', *Journal of the Society of Architectural Historians* 62 (2003), pp. 176–77.

104 McKellar, 'Architectural History', p. 159.

105 William Whyte, in *Howard Montague* [sic] *Colvin*, pp. 23–6.

106 This is a theme that is attracting increasing interest. In addition to works already cited by Arnold and McKellar, see, for example, Andrew Ballantyne, 'Architecture as Evidence', in Dana Arnold, A. A. Orgut, and B. T. Özkaya, eds., *Rethinking Architectural Historiography* (London, 2006), pp. 36–49; Iain Borden and Jane Rendell, 'From Chamber to Transformer: epistemological challenges in the methodology of theorised architectural history', *Journal of Architecture* 5 (2000), pp. 215–28; William Whyte, 'How Do Buildings Mean? Some issues of interpretation in the history of architecture', *History and Theory* 45 (2006) pp. 153–77.

Chapter Two

WITH ORDNANCE SURVEY IN HAND AND DICTIONARY IN KNAPSACK

John Harris

I begin this memoir in late April 1954 aged 23, working in Collin & Winslow's antique shop on the Fulham Road, when I was getting a grip on architectural history. 1954 was a year of an *embarrass de richesse* for antique dealers. Every antique or junk shop in Britain was stuffed with furniture and objects that today would be marked up for West End auction rooms. The Winslow name was based on Wren's Winslow Hall, Buckinghamshire, bought by Geoffrey Houghton Brown in 1948, saving it from the demolition contractors. Through the friendship of Geoffrey with inspectors in the Ministry of Works, Winslow had received one of the first Historic Building Council grants. I had to open it up every Friday for the weekend trade, and my very first task was to attend Major Ralph Verney's auction on 7 May 1954 at nearby Claydon House, a sale prior to being taken over by the National Trust. In retrospect it was a disaster sale, ignorantly lotted up. Geoffrey bought a Louis XV bureau plat for £190 which turned out to be signed by Charles Cressent with a Meudon inventory mark; but more to the point, unlotted at the end, were eight Grand Tour cork models, a pile of carvings by the genius Lightfoot, a dozen full length broken-framed family portraits laid out in a pile, and a portfolio of drawings. Of the last, in my catalogue £2.5s is penciled in. The portfolio contained Thomas Cundy's designs for Middleton Park, a set of records of antique statues in some Italian gallery, coloured engravings of Raphael's stanza, a design for a grand early eighteenth-century church monument, and a proof engraving of the interior of the Ranelagh Rotunda. It was my first purchase of architectural records.

Geoffrey introduced me to the fledgling National Buildings Record, then in Onslow Gardens, South Kensington, and I soon became a familiar there, and I must confess, I may be the only survivor of those who knew the Record then. It was there I first met Maurice Craig. I saw on the NBR desk a copy of a *Dictionary of English Architects*, by someone called H. M. Colvin, and very soon I bought my copy in Foyles, Charing Cross Road, and wrote to Mr Colvin at St John's College, informing him of these drawings. Promptly I received a reply in what I would soon come to recognize as his miniscule handwriting, the first of an exchange that would last for more than fifty-five years. I soon learned he never used a typewriter, and later that even a word processor was unmentionable. In that reply I was enjoined to write to Rupert Gunnis at Hungershall Lodge, Tunbridge Wells, *apropos* the monument design. I did so, and of course my warm reception there is related in my *No Voice from the Hall.*

By 1956 when through James Lees-Milne I had joined the RIBA Library, it was impossible not to have contrasted these two friends, who were like chalk and cheese. Rupert was patrician, but was not an archivist or documentalist in the manner of Howard, as betrayed by his *Dictionary of Sculptors*, where many sources are not given, or prove not to be what they should have been. However, unlike Howard his conversation sparkled; he was ebullient in gossip, had scant respect for dull scholars, and could be wickedly critical. His collections were arrayed in an aesthetic ambience; the scents of hot-house flowers were always in his rooms, and his great antiquarian library was there for reference and discussion. Lunch was served by Kemal, his Cypriot friend in full Turkish fig, and the afternoons were spent visiting the local nobs: Lord De L'Isle at Penshurst or Nellie Ionides at Buxted. He was *au fait* with noblemen and landed gentry throughout England, and when travelling with Howard this effected their access to country house muniment rooms. I think it telling that I heard more about those tours from Rupert than from Howard, for oddly Howard was not adept at reminiscence, although it was Howard who told me about their first visit to Calke Abbey one Sunday morning knowing that they would then get into the church. It is a story that has passed into legend. They found the iron gate to the churchyard locked, waited, and to their astonishment there arrived a few celebrants and the parson, who proceeded to squeeze themselves through a space between iron railings and a hedge because Mr Jenny, the owner of Calke, refused to unlock the gate.

Visiting Howard in Plantation Road was a different experience to that at Hungershall Lodge. Reticence might sum it up. Howard was a listener, enjoying my tales, fictional or otherwise, and giggles were few. A conservative lunch would be produced by an attentive Christina who kept her distance from the discussions in the sitting room-cum-library, and there was always the regulation visit to examine the plants in the garden, notably Alpines that I loathed! Question time increased in intensity as the RIBA Drawings Collection became progressively sorted out and catalogued. I turned recently to the second edition of the *Dictionary* of 1978 to read that he acknowledged 'the late Rupert Gunnis, my genial ally in many joint expeditions in search of architectural records', and I confess blushingly, that 'no one has contributed more information – or imparted it with more generosity, than Mr John Harris'.

During the last decade of Howard's life, Richard Hewlings and I formed the Notes and Queries Group, meeting every three months around a questions and answers lunch, often inviting fellow historians such as Mark Girouard, Geoffrey Tyack, Tim Knox, or Frank Salmon to attend. Howard would preside. He had a certain look in judging the quality of the offerings or the opinions given. There was a knowing smile for the average and raised eyebrows for the significant. Emotion was in his eyebrows. God help the correspondent who unwittingly offered information on an architect or building that had already been incorporated in his dictionary. Archival precision was a determinant in his professional life. Not even John Summerson was exempt from criticism. Indeed, without such stringency the great *Dictionary* could never have existed. In the making of his history there was no room for guesswork, and the evidence for an attribution must be over-whelming. In one letter he expressed rare humour in addressing me as The Great Attributor. I recollect my difficulties in persuading him to relent on a stylistic attribution, not least one referring to James Gibbs. Despite my passionate discourse that Hall Place, Maidenhead, a severe astylar brick house with one of the finest group of baroque chimney pieces in England, could not be more Gibbsian, and my triumphant discovery that the only architectural books in the Hall Place library catalogue were Gibbs's *Rules for Drawing* and his *Book of Architecture*, to which the owner subscribed, he would not permit its inclusion in the Dictionary. It was the same with Rotherwas in Herefordshire, typically Gibbsian with Gibbs's interiors, and again for a subscriber. As we all now recognize, in the historiography of architectural history, the *Dictionary* was a watershed. There was a before and after Colvin, for his trawling through the archive offices of Britain led to an archival explosion, and remember this was long before Google and the Internet. No other country can claim such a dictionary as one of the tools of the profession of architectural history. The comment by Rudolf Wittkower at Columbia University, who when in London had been intending to write a book on Lord Burlington, is telling: 'I must do all my research again due to that young man in Oxford'.

Howard had two strengths: he had inherited the old tradition of architectural history being written by architects, a generation that employed stylistic analysis based upon the physical study of buildings, typified by the writings of say Reginald Blomfield, J. A. Gotch or Arthur T. Bolton, to which Howard pioneered using the tools of this new archival professionalism. However, he was not alone, for he had acknowledged the editors of the Wren Society, and more to the point, Francis Sheppard's editorship of the *Survey of London* which employed distinguished historians such as Peter Bezodis, Walter Ison, and W. A. Eden, all of whom were careful documentalists; and then, we must surely recollect Summerson's *Nash* of 1935, a very modern biography. Naturally Howard's *Dictionary* created a certain mindset in the making of architectural history, focusing upon archives as the Great Game, but sometimes at the expense of the broader picture.

As my memoir seems to be broadening out into a general view of Howard as historian and his personality, his role as a teacher cannot be neglected. It is not enough to comment that one enjoyed his lectures. What mattered in the environment of Oxford and architectural history was the difficulty that young aspiring graduates found when mentored by Howard. He never realized that a student needed a continuum of advice. Many dropped by the wayside. In any case, it had never been easy in Oxford, unlike Cambridge, where due to the brilliance and initiatives of Michael Jaffé the University became a power house for the production of architectural historians. At the end of his life Howard often commented that students of the younger generation were loath to spend time in archive offices. I think he sensed that due to the loathed new art (and architectural) history, his archival architectural history was in decline. He confessed that even when advanced to doctoral status, aspirants could be ignorant of the vocabulary of architecture. His obsession with documentary veracity explains his confession to me that he found it difficult to write about garden history because gardens are evolutionary, and can be ephemeral. It is telling that neither he nor Gunnis, when working through archives, recorded gardeners or garden designers. Many articles in *Garden History* are missing from Howard's references. In Howard's consummately-edited *History of the King's Works* there is an imbalance between the documentation of the buildings and those for garden and park.

Howard and his role as a conservationist and preservationist is a very sticky matter. There have been many instances in the past forty years, and I am thinking particularly of battles fought by SAVE subsequent to its founding in 1975, that as a doyen of our profession, and as one of the three architectural knights, Howard was reluctant to put his name in support of endangered buildings. He claimed, and I quote, 'I manipulate behind the scenes', meaning his position on the Historic Buildings Council and other Establishment committees. He eschewed controversy, and I think that a pity because Sir John Summerson as a protector of our historic built environment was a busted flush.

Let me close with Map In Hand, if not with a heavy *Dictionary* in my knapsack, to evoke travelling with Howard. He demanded perfection in map-reading. If he regarded me as the best of map readers, he knew that I had used Ordnance Survey maps since the age of fourteen, first with my uncle Sid, later when hitch-hiking. Howard was very demanding, no false 'next right, then the lane on the left'. I could name at least two distinguished historians whom Howard thought quite the worst of map readers.

When travelling with Howard there was always a reason for so doing. He would rarely do a hit and run, unless knowing the occupant of the house. Not for him the experience of being driven by Gervase Jackson Stops between Northampton and Powis Castle when we made twenty-one hit and runs. However, no drive was sacrosanct that led to a ruined house or the site of a demolished one, and once there he would explore every nook and cranny.

I think we first went travelling in 1957, this to introduce him to what I call Uncle Sid country in south Bucks. We made for Iver, and the ravishing Bridgefoot House – before it was rudely cut off by the M25; then to examine the garden walls of demolished Huntsmoor Park and its island of weirs; then to Iver Grove, open to all, the ravishing Georgian neo-classic blue and white glass then still in its staircase, later taken out by the Ministry of Works when they compulsorily acquired the house. The glass has never been seen to this day. Then to Round Coppice, where Lord Burlington had built a villa for Lord Bruce, and on to Langley Park, when we stopped to see the Kedermister Library in Langley church, and circled back towards Iver via Richings Park, the house demolished, but all around ruinous by wartime occupants. All we could discover of this famous Switzerian garden were many ancient trees.

A more typical day's outing was an early one in 1960. I had been working on the Burlington Devonshire catalogue, and was intrigued by the Hollar etching of Basing Castle showing indistinctly a classical giant order, for I could recollect an incident when hitch-hiking to Dorset in 1949 just before National Service, being dumped off by a farmer at Basing, so I made a bee-line for the castle mounds. Within the enclosure a brick gazebo housed a museum of bits and pieces, and lying about on the grassy sward were half a dozen beautiful pilaster capitals. Of course, I knew nothing then about Inigo. This memory I later communicated to Howard, so a day was organized, and we met up at Basingstoke railway station, Howard bringing Christina's routine chicken fricassé picnic. At Basing we were in agreement that the capitals could have been by Jones, so classical were they. But should the likes of Gordon Higgott take a measure to them, alas they are no longer there, for some idiotic authority scooped them up for landfill.

After Basing we made for Kempshott Park, for I had that very year of 1960 seen the Kempshott Park room in the museum at St Louis, and I expounded to Howard my Henry Holland theory – designs in the Royal Library, I claiming that at least one room there was by Holland for the Prince Regent, whose hunting lodge it was. I wrote about this the following year as quite one of the finest neo-classic rooms in the USA; but in 1988 I had to eat my words, and wrote about the same room under the title, 'The Room that Never Was', for except for some wallpaper and one chimney piece, it was pure invention in 1930, the doorcases coming from Lincolnshire. Howard was not one for 'Up – Over – and In', but I wriggled my way through a window, and unbolted a door. The house still had two rooms in Holland's style, and should have been in Howard's *Dictionary*, as the evidence was strong, especially as the saloon chimney piece was one of three commissioned in Rome for the Prince Regent in 1795 from the great British sculptor John Deare. Alas, this evidence was not enough for Howard, no archives, no entry!

From Kempshott we dropped down to Stratton Park where Howard had secured entry from the Baring Estate Office, about to demolish the house. We could deduce how Dance had worked over the Palladian house built in 1731 by John Sanderson. Sadly, like Bowood, it was a house unloved by its owner, who commissioned its successor, the wretched leaky modern house that I can now demean, as its litigious modernist architect is now dead. Of course, on our tour the Grange followed, and I and Marcus Binney were yet to confront Basher Baring's cohorts in the Winchester Courts, where we won the battle for its retention, ultimately thanks to Joe Crook spilling the beans to the President of the Council for Europe at the opening of the Neo-classic exhibition, when it was announced that The Grange was about to be blown up. On this day at The Grange we picnicked on Abbotstone Down, where old outbuildings brought forth discussion about the precocious Palladian hunting lodge built here for the first Duke of Bolton, and we also recollected the vast house proposed by James Gibbs for the second Duke in the 1730s, and agreed there was a need for an archaeological survey. Then on the return it was tea at Herriard Park with the Jervoises's to see John James's wooden model, and hear their laments that they wanted to live in a bungalow. They got their way when they needlessly demolished their house in 1965. We had now made a circuit, and were once more on the edge of Basingstoke, where pausing at Hackwood Park I tried to convince Howard that the late seventeenth-century house there was by William Talman.

For longer tours, say of three days and two nights, Howard was partial to cosy inns, many identified in the then old-fashioned *Good Food Guide*. It was essential to have a fire in the bar. This introduced me to a Howard fad, to carry a roll of brown paper and a box of drawing pins, for he hated light coming through his bedroom window. One correspondent has remarked that he often stowed a small mattress in the car. For one night in the mid-1960s we stayed in the Mason's Arms at Knowstone on the Somerset-Dorset borders, somehow well-named, as we were looking at a group of houses by J. T. Knowles all within a few miles of each other in what you might call Fourth Earl of Egremont country: the stables at the lost 1838 Silverton; then Blackborough House, also 1838 for Lord Egremont, the site not yet a car dump; then Thorndon of 1844; and finally Kentisbeare of 1841 for Lord Egremont's brother. This tour led us to Escot to see if anything survived from the fire of 1808 that destroyed this house shown in *Vitruvius Britannicus*, later discovered to be by the Wrennite William Taylor.

On another tour, a Dorset one in the seventies, there were certain erudite determinants, although I suppose there always were such determinents: what date was the Spalatro capital at Whatcombe? Was James Frampton's 1744 Palladian villa at Moreton by Roger Morris, because it incorporated Morrisonian details, such as the Marble Hill and Lydiard Tregoze fanlight? Or is Merly really an amateur's house built by Ralph Willett for himself? Howard thought Thomas Cartwright a better guess. We saw Wimborne St Giles House, before the vicissitudes that afflicted the Earl of Shaftesbury, later murdered in the south of France by one of his molls. The renaissance bronze statuette attributed to Antico was still there as a door stop to the saloon; but of course much earlier Howard and Rupert had only been given a cursory look at the family archive, and the discoveries made by Susanna Fleming about the garden and the role of Henry Flitcroft were in the future, as was the degradation of the house and garden buildings. The inn that night was the Piddle at Piddletrentide; very cosy, fires in the bar, and an agreeable dinner. Next morning Howard commented that I looked tired. In fact I was haggard, but I never dared to tell him that my night was restless because on the other side of a thin partition a lusty young couple were bonking throughout the night. Now had I told this to Rupert, there would have been a great guffaw, but Howard's eyebrows would have probably fluttered in embarrassment.

Chapter Three

HOWARD COLVIN'S *UNBUILT OXFORD* AND THE 'MIGHT-HAVE-BEENS' OF ARCHITECTURAL HISTORY

Frank Salmon

In one sense Howard Colvin's *Unbuilt Oxford,* which he published in 1983, is the most unusual and uncharacteristic of all his books (Fig. 3.1). Having been trained as an historian, by the 1980s Colvin had developed a reputation second-to-none for applying rigorous standards of evidential proof to the record of architecture in the successive editions of his *Biographical Dictionary of British Architects* and in his own contributions to, and editorship of, *The History of the King's Works,* eschewing the sort of speculations that accompany the fictive and the frankly preposterous. *Unbuilt Oxford,* which he must have written not long after the crucial second edition of the *Biographical Dictionary* appeared in 1978 and when the 1982 final volume of *The King's Works* was in press, was prepared without the full apparatus of footnotes to give source or corroborative information (although Colvin simply could not resist parenthesising one reference within the text and twenty asterisked footnotes do creep in among the 187 pages). This was the book, in other words, with which, academically-speaking, Howard Colvin finally let his hair down at what (for him) was the relatively tender age of 64. In it he also indulged himself in rare instances of levity in print, such as when explaining the absence of any work in Oxford by Inigo Jones or John Webb by saying of the seventeenth-century dons that 'art and intellect, if not actually estranged, were hardly on terms of intimacy' – or, when accounting for the unaccountable 1930s use of Cotswold-style rubble walls at Giles Gilbert Scott's New Bodleian Library by describing the building as 'like a dinner jacket made of Harris tweed'.[1]

In another sense, however, *Unbuilt Oxford* may be seen as classic Colvin. Dealing as it does with the university that had, by the time of its publication, been the base of his operations for some 35 years, it demonstrates admirably the great judgement that can be acquired by long study of one architectural ambience and by close knowledge of its archival sources. Indeed, the book is a masterpiece of deep familiarity with a place and with its architectural culture – something increasingly uncommon in an age of smash-and-grab scholarship that has arisen, in academia at least, to meet the requirements of research assessment exercises and

[1] Howard Colvin, *Unbuilt Oxford* (New Haven and London, 1983), pp. 9, 178.

Fig. 3.1: Howard Colvin: *Unbuilt Oxford* (Yale University Press, 1983), front cover.

promotions committees. The book also serves to remind us of something about Colvin that is in danger of being forgotten: that he was deeply interested in buildings themselves as well as in the records that refer to them. Many members of the Society of Architectural Historians of Great Britain will recall that, well into his 70s, Colvin was a frequent presence at residential county annual conferences, keen to take advantage of the *entrée* to a house or chapel he had not seen before or had not studied for a long time

As those who knew him will aver, Colvin was a modest man who wore his extraordinary knowledge lightly and who was not given to autobiographical declarations or to methodological introspection in his writings. *Unbuilt Oxford* opens, however, by drawing a clear distinction – one we may perhaps infer to have been a defining one in his own intellectual journey – between the historian and the architectural historian. 'The might-have-beens of history', Colvin wrote

> are not popular with historians. Why something did not happen may be a proper subject for historical inquiry, but a hypothetical train of events is emphatically not. For the architectural historian, however, the might-have-beens of his subject are in a rather different category. Buildings that failed to get erected are a perfectly legitimate subject of inquiry, for many of them exist on paper, and we can often evaluate them as well as we can existing buildings, not to mention destroyed ones. Moreover, unlike the military and the political might-have-beens, the architectural ones often represent a genuine choice that offered itself at the time – a choice between rival architects, between different styles, between different interpretations of the same style. So, by studying these rejected alternatives we can gain a better idea of the reasons that determined the final choice, and see more clearly the place of a given building in architectural history.[2]

As a personal aside, I must confess that this justification for detailed study of architecture that never made it beyond the drafting table has always held great appeal for me. In the mid-1980s, when Colvin made this statement, I was hard at work in Florence for my Master's dissertation on the two possible sites for the Laurentian Library rejected by Michelangelo before he built it in its present location.[3] I well remember the bemusement of the elderly German gentleman who was supporting an impoverished student by providing me with accommodation and who, at the end of each of my days of hard labour in the archives, would bait me with the thickly accented question: 'So Frank, what did you discover today that Michelangelo decided *not* to build?' But Colvin was quite right, of course. In architectural history, designs that failed to get erected are an important subject of study and the reasons why they did not, when pursued thoroughly, are always

2 Ibid., p. vi.

3 See Frank Salmon, 'The Site of Michelangelo's Laurentian Library', *Journal of the Society of Architectural Historians* 49 (1990), pp. 407–29.

Fig. 3.2: J. Drayton Wyatt (engraved by I. S. Heaviside): Perspective of design with flêche for the new Chapel of St John's College, Cambridge, by George Gilbert Scott (from *The Builder*, 28 March, 1863, p. 225).

more instructive than a hypothetical train of other kinds of historical events that did not occur because of a single decision taken at the start. Moreover, it soon becomes apparent to the reader of *Unbuilt Oxford* that the word 'unbuilt' may take on a number of different meanings in architectural history. Certainly it can refer to speculative designs or competition drawings for buildings that were never destined to exist or which were ultimately built by someone else. But it also refers to those parts of buildings that were left incomplete when construction *did* take place, as in the case of the spectral nave of Merton College Chapel – which Colvin used perceptively to explain that peculiar Oxford tradition of chapels with transepts across the entrance end. Or it can refer to ideas abandoned by the architect during the design process, as in the elevation by Hawksmoor for a concave façade between the towers at All Souls. Or 'unbuilt' can refer to specific parts of buildings that, for whatever reason, were changed between the design and construction stages, as can be seen in the case of the Chapel of my own college, St John's in Cambridge, where George Gilbert Scott's accepted scheme, as published in *The Builder* in 1863, featured a surmounting flêche ultimately to be replaced by the enormous tower that the College could not resist when a donor of 'princely munificence' offered to pay for it in 1864, even though construction was already in progress (Fig. 3.2).[4]

Of course these issues of what was built and what was not pertain in all kinds of architectural contexts. I suspect that the specific idea of making a case study of Oxford came to Colvin as a result of his long engagement with visualising the lost, the much altered and the never built in *The History of the King's Works*. Oxford is, however, a very particular context – one that might be compared in its nature only with England's other University of medieval origin. For all their differences, Oxford and Cambridge present far more similarities in terms of architectural history, as has long been recognised. Scott, for example, was careful to establish with the fellows of St John's College Cambridge that their new Chapel would be a distinctive work, but he was explicit in saying that the model for its western transept arrangement was the unusual Oxford model that has its origin at Merton.[5] He also compared it with his own earlier Chapel at Exeter College; and he justified the addition of a tower of such scale at St John's by reference to that of Magdalen College Oxford.[6] Colvin certainly appreciated the symbiotic relationship that exists between the architectural histories of the two universities. On the first page of *Unbuilt Oxford* he commented on the absence of any Oxonian document to match Henry VI's plan for King's College Cambridge, and there are more comparisons with Cambridge throughout the book than there are with any other place, London included. This is not to say, however, that a book on *Unbuilt Cambridge* was a 'might-have-been' for Howard himself. After completing *Unbuilt Oxford* he continued to produce work that stemmed from deep familiarity with his own University (these being the books on Canterbury Quadrangle at his own St John's College and on the architecture of All Souls), only ranging further afield for his final monograph *Architecture and the Afterlife*, published in 1991. I doubt that Howard would have regarded himself as sufficiently knowledgeable about either the specifics or the general contexts of the Cambridge situation to produce a parallel study to *Unbuilt Oxford* – which is, after all, a narrative history of the University itself as seen from the vantage point of architectural debates, commissions and failures.

The purpose of my essay, therefore, is not to speculate what a book by Colvin entitled *Unbuilt Cambridge* might have been like, for that would be to fall precisely into the trap of presenting a hypothetical historical occurrence of the type that Colvin himself counselled against. I want instead to explore a few issues of research and explication that *Unbuilt Oxford* raises against the contexts of

[4] *Builder* 21 (1863), p. 225. See also Alec Crook, *From the Foundation to Gilbert Scott: A History of the Buildings of St John's College, Cambridge* (Cambridge, 1980), p. 100.

[5] Crook, *From the Foundation*, p. 95.

[6] Ibid., pp. 96 and 101.

Cambridge, in order to evaluate both the advantages and risks of such an approach. Before doing that, however, it is worth pausing a moment to consider the commercial implications of publications of this type – something that is often overlooked when more academic questions are under consideration. In this case, the writing style and relative lack of scholarly apparatus were surely part of a plan to produce a book for a wider market than would normally be the case with such detailed architectural history. This evidently worked, for the original hardback of *Unbuilt Oxford* quickly sold out and it then went into paperback, selling an overall total of some 5000 copies in the UK and 3000 in the USA. That is probably more than all four editions of Colvin's indispensable *Biographical Dictionary* put together.[7] Today, of course, a publisher would make *Unbuilt Oxford* (for which Colvin was permitted only seven colour plates and a modest format, significantly smaller than A4) still more attractive. Indeed, a book on *Unbuilt Cambridge* would require plentiful illustration to augment the histories of the college and university buildings laid out in Robert Willis's and John Willis Clark's masterly three-volume *Architectural History of the University of Cambridge* of 1886, for which there is no Oxford equivalent.

Whilst no one would contest the fact that the universities and colleges of both Oxford and Cambridge have intrinsically rich architectural histories in and of themselves, the first question that arises is whether these can and should be treated in isolation from their surrounding city contexts. In *Unbuilt Oxford,* Colvin specifically excluded road- and town-planning schemes for the City, with the exception of a paragraph on Hawksmoor's scheme to remodel the area around the Bodleian. The Shire Hall and Town Hall competitions of 1837 and 1891 respectively are the only ones he mentions which were entirely in the remit of the city authorities. In a number of other instances, however, he was compelled to include city buildings because of the involvement of people connected with the University. Without the church of All Saints on the High, for example, the story of Dean Henry Aldrich as architect and patron in Oxford would not have been complete, for Aldrich was a Trustee for the rebuilding and probably designed it – although in a number of important respects, including the steeple, his ideas were not followed. A century later the Provost of Oriel College was involved in the foundation of Oxford's 1819 Commissioners'-style church of St Martin at Carfax, and Colvin also mentioned the two city churches built under the inspiration of Tractarian dons. Consideration was needed, too, of the effects of town developments on gown. The opening up of Beaumont Street in the 1820s, for example (albeit the idea of the then Rector of Lincoln College), exposed afresh the nondescript frontage of Worcester College. The fellows of Worcester were

[7] Gillian Malpass of Yale University Press, London, kindly provided me with this information.

provoked to commission new designs – from the Oxford architect Daniel Robertson in 1827 for a grand Roman portico somewhat in the manner of Robert Adam's Osterley and, in 1837, as an early example of his Italianate style complete with Belvedere and lantern, from Charles Barry.[8]

It is arguable that in Cambridge, still more than in Oxford, the interaction of town and gown forms a fundamental aspect of the architectural identity of the whole place. Is there anywhere else in England where we find so relatively small a municipality dominated by so relatively large a private institution? Moreover, street and college are more fully integrated even than in Oxford. There is no street situation in Cambridge where one can walk and see nothing but University buildings, as one can in circumnavigating the Radcliffe Camera. Hawkmoor's Oxford plan could make the Bodleian area a 'Forum Universitatis' – and develop a separate 'Forum Civitatis' to the west at Carfax. In Cambridge, by contrast, there could be but one Forum – and that only achieved by demolishing the shops clustered on what is today King's Parade and replacing them with a pair of large edifices, depicted as a version of the Clarendon Building in Gordon Cullen's 1955 hypothetical perspective of Hawksmoor's scheme (Figs. 3.3–5). In Hawksmoor's plan, the great new vista from Christ's College through to King's College Chapel cuts across the Market – which is given added dignity through a screen of columns – and the 'port triumpll' gateway at the corner of Parker's Piece is the entrance to the central part of the whole town, not just the University. It might be wondered how useful a piece of architectural history a volume on *Unbuilt Cambridge* would be if the contexts provided by, for example, Sir William Holford's plan for the city of 1950 were to be excluded.

The next question I want to raise concerns the decisions that Colvin took about the structure to be adopted for *Unbuilt Oxford*. In the obituary that appeared in the *Independent* newspaper, Richard Hewlings reported that Colvin – whom he knew very well – considered Willis's *Architectural History of the University of Cambridge* as his 'intellectual model' and that he believed this work to be 'almost faultless'.[9] It will be recalled that the first two volumes of Willis's history proceed on a college-by-college basis, chronologically in order of foundation from Peterhouse to Downing. The third volume examined the much smaller number of University Buildings and then presented a series of taxonomic essays on the component parts of a college, drawing in much comparative evidence from Oxford examples, in fact. Willis's work, however, extends to over two thousand pages and to have proceeded on a college-by-college basis would

8 Colvin, *Unbuilt Oxford*, p. 58, gave the date of 1827 for Barry's design in a typographical slip to the caption for fig. 59.

9 Richard Hewlings, 'Sir Howard Colvin', *Independent* 1 January 2008, p. 34.

Fig. 3.3–5. Gordon Cullen: three views of the University Forum from *The Town of Cambridge as it Ought to be Reformed: The Plan of Nicholas Hawksmoor Interpreted in an Essay by David Roberts* (Cambridge University Press, 1955); 3.3 (above): The University Forum, existing view; 3.4 (below): The University Forum, as envisaged by Hawksmoor; Fig. 3.5 (opposite): The Forum seen from the Market Place, as envisaged by Hawksmoor.

have been wholly impracticable for a book of the size and scope of *Unbuilt Oxford*. Colvin might have adopted a typological approach – perhaps dealing, as Willis had done, with the component parts of colleges: chapels, halls, libraries, and so on. But this would have meant sacrificing much of the historical nuances that stem from the idiosyncratic ideas and behaviour of dons for, as all Oxbridge insiders know well, no two colleges are quite alike in their intellectual and practical habits.

The underpinning structure of *Unbuilt Oxford* is therefore chronological – notwithstanding that this resulted in some imbalance between the first five hundred years of the University's history, for which little evidence of the unbuilt survives, and the most recent three hundred years for which there is almost too great a preponderance of evidence. This approach, however, allowed strengths in the narrative to emerge without forcing Colvin to deal in any detail with the weaknesses. And, under the overall umbrella of chronology, he was able to develop typologies. Thus we have two chapters that have stylistic labels (although most scholars of sixteenth-century British architecture would now baulk at the notion of a 'Retarded Renaissance' in this country) and the final chapter is not exclusively about the 'Modern Movement'. Then there are the chapters that centre on patrons and the academic-architect, that is to say those on the Oxonian Archbishop of Canterbury Gilbert Sheldon (who exemplified 'The Limits of a Private Purse') and on Dr George Clarke. Individual architects of special importance to Oxford – Hawksmoor, Pugin, and Jackson – appear in chapters of their own. There is the single chapter that takes building typology as its key: that on the Ashmolean and Oxford Museums. Finally, Magdalen College is singled out for special treatment – given this dubious honour because, as Colvin put it, having extracted designs from more than twenty architects between 1720 and 1844, it had a 'longer history of architectural indecision than any other Oxford college'.[10] By way of compensation, however, a detail from Humphry Repton's Red Book design for Magdalen of 1800–1801, showing the College against a lake formed from the River Cherwell, was awarded pride of place on the front cover of *Unbuilt Oxford*.

Let us stick with rivers, and consider how a volume on *Unbuilt Cambridge* might row competitively alongside *Unbuilt Oxford* rather as the two universities do on the Tideway each year. As Colvin pointed out, the masons of sixteenth-century Oxford have no intellectual figure of the calibre of Cambridge's John Caius to direct their architectural endeavours. In the seventeenth century, however, Oxford begins to draw level: Wren does not get to build the Sheldonian quite as he intended. Here Colvin deployed Paul Draper (Fig. 3.6), one of two artist- draftsmen he used for his book, to visualise how the Theatre might have looked with attached Ionic columns and tall first-floor windows – borrowed, perhaps, from the upper floor of the Library at Trinity College, Cambridge – for which Wren's first idea, of a circular library at the river end of Nevile's Court remained unbuilt (as did his design for a Senate House in Cambridge).[11] The two universities remain level with Gibbs, but Oxford pulls decidedly ahead with Hawksmoor's astonishing sequence of designs for All Souls, Magdalen, Queen's, Brasenose, Worcester, and the Radcliffe Camera. Towards the end of the eighteenth century Cambridge comes back into it with Robert Adam's designs for the completion of King's College and for a new University Library to the north of King's Chapel, incorporating Gibbs's Senate House.[12] In the early-nineteenth

[10] Colvin, *Unbuilt Oxford*, p. 78.

[11] See Howard Colvin, 'The Building', in David McKitterick, ed., *The Making of the Wren Library* (Cambridge, 1995), pp. 30–33 and figures 18, 24, 28–31; Anthony Geraghty, *The Architectural Drawings of Sir Christopher Wren at All Souls College, Oxford: a complete catalogue* (Aldershot, 2007), pp. 27–34.

[12] See Allan Doig, *The Architectural Drawings Collection of King's College, Cambridge: a catalogue and historical synopsis of the major project drawings of the eighteenth and nineteenth centuries* (Avebury, 1979), pp. 31–32 and plates 12–13; and Alistair Rowan, *'Bob the Roman': heroic antiquity and the architecture of Robert Adam* (London, 2003), pp. 32, 38.

Fig. 3.6. Paul Draper: conjectural drawing of Christopher Wren's possible intentions for the Sheldonian Theatre, Oxford, from Howard Colvin, *Unbuilt Oxford* (1983), page 17.

century the light blue boat of Cambridge edges ahead. William Wilkins's Greek Revival Downing College of 1804 onwards, even lacking its unbuilt Doric propylaeum and grandiose Ionic Chapel and Library range (Fig. 3.7), still represents a turning point in the history of British architecture nationally and, as Colvin pointed out, Oxford had little to match the sequence of Cambridge competitions that ensued in the 1820s and 30s for King's College, New Court at St John's, the Pitt Press, the University Library, and the Fitzwilliam Museum. By the second half of the nineteenth century, the High Victorian powerhouses are at full throttle in the middle of both boats. From Cambridge's point of view, we should be relieved that King's College did not proceed to act upon the results of its 1877 competition that saw Gilbert Scott, William Burges, and G. E. Street proffer massive three-storey residential blocks and gatehouses to replace Wilkins's neo-Perpendicular screen confection, merely fifty years old.[13] Cambridge college façades are of brick – or of brick refaced in ashlar in the eighteenth century – and in consequence generally quite flat in profile. They do not have the same dynamic relationship with the streets as do Oxford's stone-built colleges, with their surface rhythms of bays and oriels and rooftop profusion of gables and dormers. Scott's perspective, moreover, shows the proposed new building for King's at an angle and distance from which it could never have been seen (Fig. 3.8). In reality its scale on the street would have been overpowering and would have caused the destruction of one of the finest, crescendoing pieces of street scenography anywhere in England.

The boats row on into the twentieth century and the coxes are becoming angry with their crews. Colvin castigates Oxford dons for losing the ability to judge designs and for having minds 'attuned to beauties other than architectural'. He wonders whether it might have been 'worthwhile sacrificing the gloomy Master's Lodgings' of Balliol for the uncompromising Tecton-inspired dining hall on Broad Street.[14] Meanwhile, in 1964 Nicholas Taylor and Philip Booth berate Christ's College, Cambridge which, they say portentously, 'will be remembered in architectural history for having turned down Walter Gropius in 1937' (referring to Gropius's and Fry's proposed Hobson Street building), before begrudgingly admitting that the College did later build part of Denis Lasdun's Brutalist 'Typewriter' building.[15] After the war, the boats find the right current again – in no small part due to the role played by Colvin himself in ousting Sir Edward Maufe at his own St John's College in favour of Michael Powers of the Architects Co-Partnership and their 'Beehive' building. However, Oxford's St Catherine's College by Jacobsen is more than matched by Cambridge's

[13] Doig, *The Architectural Drawings Collection of King's College, Cambridge*, pp. 63–71 and plates 43–53.

[14] Colvin, *Unbuilt Oxford*, pp. 159 and 161.

[15] Nicholas Taylor and Philip Booth, *Cambridge New Architecture* (London, 1970), pp. 14–15.

Fig. 3.7. R. B. Harraden after William Wilkins (etched by Elizabeth Byrne): Proposed entrance to Downing College, Cambridge (1809).

Fig. 3.8. George Gilbert Scott: Perspective view to north-west of Design 'A' for east front of King's College, Cambridge, competition entry of 1877 (Courtesy of King's College, Cambridge: GGS III 4).

Fitzwilliam, New Hall, and Churchill Colleges. Along the way, James Stirling does not win the 1958 competition for Churchill with his fortress like design, nor does he get to build the faceted glass wall of student rooms projected for Selwyn College the next year. But in the mid-1960s he does get to launch a full-frontal Postmodern assault on Casson and Conder's doctrinaire Raised Faculty Building when he wins the competition to design the History Faculty Building.

What I hope I have shown by this little analogy of the Boat Race as applied to the unbuilt is that the architectural histories of the two universities have moved in parallel streams, but have not necessarily moved at the same time. The same is true of another important aspect of their architectural cultures – the intellectual or ideological composition of those academic men (and much more recently women) who commissioned or judged architectural designs. Between them the two universities boast some remarkable figures in this regard, but they rarely overlap chronologically. Thus in the sixteenth century, as we have already seen, Oxford had no one to match John Caius. In the early eighteenth century Cambridge was quite without a Henry Aldrich or George Clarke. And in the middle of the nineteenth century Oxford did not really have a William Whewell or a Robert Willis (the Tractarians naturally held strong views on architecture, but these were driven by religious ideology.) Of course Aldrich and Clarke, as architectural connoisseurs – the first of whom even took up the dividers – were different types of men from the proto-architectural historians Whewell and Willis, who stood at the forefront of scholarship and architectural taxonomy rather than at the cutting edge of design. But the point is that whilst these men were around their universities, the standard of architectural knowledge and debate was very high. In *Unbuilt Oxford* Colvin laments the loss of such a level of architectural appreciation amongst Oxford academics in the twentieth century, but Cambridge fared rather better, even somewhat reluctantly creating a Department of Architecture and appointing E. H. Prior as the first Professor.[16]

It is true to say, then, that the numerous commissions and competitions that occurred in Oxford and Cambridge, particularly from the early nineteenth century and on into the second half of the twentieth, are a rich and microcosmic source of information about the condition of architecture nationally. Of course University and College commissions and/or competitions were and are effectively made by academics acting in a private capacity, and thus owing the public at large no obligation to record or to account for their decisions. But dons can be notoriously opinionated – and voluble. The minutes of the 1874 competition to

[16] See Andrew Saint, 'The Cambridge School of Architecture: A Brief History', in Tom Holbrook, ed., *Compendium: the work of the University of Cambridge Department of Architecture* (Cambridge, 2006), pp. 12–20.

design the proposed top for the bell tower at Christ Church not only record the voting of the fellows in detail but also describe some the designs in mocking terms: G. F. Bodley was said to want to place 'a leaden Pepperbox on top' and Basil Champneys's design was 'like a Mayday Garland'. Bodley was in fact the victor but, as Colvin reported it, almost every detail of his design 'had to be thrashed out with a committee by no means disposed to defer to his judgement on any single point.'[17] Some insults of this type naturally reached the press. The *Builder's* comments on rival designs for the 1854 Oxford Museum competition grouped the thirty-three entries by style, including two in a category entitled 'The Order of Confusion' and a further two in a category simply called 'Abominations'.[18]

It must have been a disagreement of extraordinary proportions that led the fellows of Balliol, in 1843, to accept their Master's decision to remove from the minutes all detail of the debate about Pugin's proposals for their College. Generally we have a lot more evidence to go on as to why decisions were taken as they were – a point of great richness in the architectural histories of the two universities. Even here, however, there is an interesting difference between them. In nineteenth-century Oxford the habit was for a committee or 'Delegacy' to be set up to organise competitions, scrutinise entries, perhaps consult with a senior architect who was not competing and then to make recommendations to Convocation as to how to vote. A very good case of this is the 1839 competition for the Ashmolean Museum (though it was also the case for the University Museum and no fewer than three delegacies were needed to secure Jackson's Examination Schools between 1869 and 1875).[19] The delegates for the Ashmolean comprised the Vice-Chancellor, three Heads of Houses, the two proctors, and eleven other members of the University. Twenty-eight entries were received; they shortlisted five and asked Robert Smirke for his opinions of these. Smirke recommended Charles Robert Cockerell, who was then unanimously chosen. A majority voted to give a second prize to the local Oxford architect John Plowman. Quite reasonably, Convocation then became anxious about the process because the delegates had no idea how much Cockerell's building would cost. The parallel case of the 1835 Fitzwilliam Museum competition in Cambridge makes a contrast

[17] Colvin, *Unbuilt Oxford*, p. 140. The date of 1873 given by Colvin for minutes and the competition designs is incorrect and Michael Hall has established that, although Bodley was preferred to T. G. Jackson by 17 votes to 9 in the committee, his real problem was that the College's Governing Body remained divided over the issue. I am very grateful to Michael Hall for having kindly shared with me the section on the Christ Church belfry from his forthcoming monograph on Bodley.

[18] Quoted by Colvin, *Unbuilt Oxford*, p. 126.

[19] I am grateful to Jon Whiteley of the Museum for information about the Ashmolean, as Colvin did not include details in *Unbuilt Oxford*.

with this. Thirty-six schemes were sent in by twenty-seven architects. These were displayed publicly and the whole Senate of the University invited to vote upon as many of them as they liked in the first of two rounds. George Basevi's ultimately successful design commanded the support of 90 per cent of the 157 members of Senate who voted. In the second round first-past-the-post applied and 175 members voted. Basevi was a clear winner with 131 votes – or 75 per cent of those cast. Not only do we learn from this something of the strength of the classical tradition in the University as exemplified by the Cambridge Hellenists at this time, we also see how little fooled large numbers of dons were by some of the more extravagant and eye-catching designs submitted to the competition.[20] Foremost among these was surely Thomas Rickman's Gothic scheme, with its preposter- ously useless tower and internal spaces – such as the view inside the Museum's supposed 'Library' which provided virtually no accommodation for books (Figs. 3.9–10).[21]

As may be judged from this example and from others that have been given here, the history of 'Unbuilt Cambridge' offers a rich a seam of material when it comes to elucidating the intellectual and cultural climate of the University, as Colvin similarly found when researching and writing *Unbuilt Oxford* thirty years ago. Whilst these seams are naturally of interest to members of the two universities, present and past, they also reflect the national situation at various significant moments in history. When coupled to the number of important architectural figures who became involved both in commissioning and designing new buildings in these two universities, studies of this type do not fall into the realm of provinciality. Finally, aside from the serious history involved in the Oxbridge architectural narrative, there is the visual and verbal fun of picking apart design schemes and donnish committees – and of giving the wider reading public an *entrée* to the weird world of the Senior 'Common' or 'Combination' Room. Perhaps, if a volume on *Unbuilt Cambridge* were to be attempted, the author might have to do more to lock the privileged world of the gown into the wider contextual one of the town than Colvin did in *Unbuilt Oxford,* but the methods and approaches that he adopted for this type of material appear to me to retain their validity today. A friend of mine tells a story of how, when discussing the novels of E. M. Forster with her family one Christmas, the talk turned to the qualities of *Howard's End.* 'Now I forget', said one of the company, 'how *does* Howard die – in the end?' We historians of British architecture must consider ourselves fortunate, I think, to have had a Howard whose end, in some of the key respects detailed in this essay, is not in sight.

[20] For a full account of the Fitzwilliam Museum competition see Frank Salmon, *Building on Ruins: the rediscovery of Rome and English architecture* (Aldershot, 2000), pp. 169–88.

[21] See also David Watkin, *The Triumph of the Classical: Cambridge architecture 1804–1834* (Cambridge, 1977), pp. 48–49 and plates 19 and 20.

Figs. 3.9–10. Thomas Rickman and Richard Charles Hussey: Drawings from Design B for the Fitzwilliam Museum, Cambridge, competition of 1834–35; Perspective view to north-west, and inset: Interior perspective of the 'Library' (both from RIBA Library, Drawings and Archives Collection).

THE CANTERBURY QUADRANGLE

ST JOHN'S COLLEGE
OXFORD

HOWARD
COLVIN

Chapter Four

AFTER COLVIN'S *CANTERBURY QUADRANGLE*[1]

Anthony Geraghty

Howard Colvin's *The Canterbury Quadrangle St John's College Oxford* is a disappointing work.[2] Published by Oxford University Press in 1988, the book began life as a lecture, given in June 1986, to commemorate the 350th anniversary of the quadrangle's completion. Why disappointing? Because the book focuses almost exclusively on the forms of the building and gives next to no consideration of the Quadrangle's place in the wider history of Caroline England. That the Quadrangle occupies such a place is beyond question, for it was conceived in 1630 and built in 1631–36 by William Laud, that determined son of a Reading clothier, who, through brute force of personality, rose to be Chancellor of Oxford, Bishop of London, and the most hated man in England. As Archbishop of Canterbury (from 1633), he played a central part in the personal rule of Charles I. It was Laud who encouraged the King in his elevated notion of monarchy, and it was Laud who devised and brutally enforced a policy of civic obedience and religious conformity. Laud executed these policies nationally, as Archbishop of Canterbury, and locally, as Chancellor of Oxford. The ancient universities, he believed, were microcosms of England, and, as such, essential to the wellbeing of England. By 1636, when the quadrangle was inaugurated in the presence of the King, these policies had reached their symbolic apogee. Oxford was apparently flourishing, having updated her statutes and renewed her charter; England and Scotland were seemingly at peace. The union of church and crown was apparent for all to see, in the reality of the King's person at St John's, and in the heraldic ornament of the quadrangle, where mitre takes its place below crown. Laud's triumph, however, was short lived. Within years he witnessed the destruction of everything he held dearest, his own neck included. But his buildings were to prevail, and the Canterbury Quadrangle keeps eloquent testimony to the first of Oxford's lost causes – her commitment to monarchy and episcopacy.[3]

1 I have given a tribute to Howard Colvin elsewhere (*The Burlington Magazine*, 150 [September 2008], pp. 613–14). This paper is less about Howard than it is the current state of architectural history in Great Britain. It is intentionally polemical, and there are of course exceptions to my generalizations, not least the scholars already producing the kind of work I advocate. They remain, however, a distinguished minority.

2 Howard Colvin, *The Canterbury Quadrangle St John's College Oxford* (Oxford, 1988).

3 H. R. Trevor-Roper, *Archbishop Laud* (London, 1962), pp. 271–94; Kevin Sharpe, 'Archbishop Laud and the University of Oxford', in H. Lloyd-Jones, V. Pearl, and B. Worden,

Fig. 4.1 (*opposite*). Howard Colvin, *The Canterbury Quadrangle* (Oxford, 1988): dustjacket

Yet, for Colvin, Laud's 'attempt to impose ... an ordered society united in obedience and loyalty to an autocratic monarchy is beyond the scope of this book' (p. 3). That there might be a relationship between the forms of the building and the nature of Laud's authoritarian policies is not considered. Instead, Colvin analyses the building in exclusively art historical terms – indeed, *The Canterbury Quadrangle* is by far and away his most art historical book, in the sense that it is primarily concerned with architectural forms, with the origins of these forms in Continental Europe, and with the attributional significance of these forms. Colvin's analysis – like everything he did – is thorough, formidably so; and his erudite discussion of the building's forms, especially its carved ornament, testifies not only to his formidable scholarship, but to a lifetime's experience of the building and the serendipity that flows from this. But it still disappoints.

Having analysed the design in these terms – though not its non-Renaissance features, which he largely ignores[4] – Colvin steers his way towards an attribution. Noting stylistic similarities between the frontispieces at St John's and a group of funerary monuments associated with the court of Charles I, Colvin posits Balthazar Gerbier as a possible architect. He then brings his analysis to a close, concluding with a statement of the frontispieces's 'place in English architectural history': 'They represent', he states, 'a baroque alternative to the Italian classicism of Inigo Jones, of which there might well have been more examples but for the Civil War ... So the Canterbury Quadrangle is not only a memorial to a great political prelate: it represents an architectural initiative that failed with the regime that he sustained' (p. 52). Architecture and politics are here juxtaposed, but only as analogy, and it is Colvin's unwillingness to probe the possibility of such a relationship that disappoints. Instead, he concludes with an art historical label – the baroque – the kind of label that he played no part in conceptualising or modifying and that seldom carries much force in his writings.

So, reading *The Canterbury Quadrangle*, one is left with a sense that Colvin was uninterested in history, which, in view of his training as a medieval historian, is unexpected. Such an assessment of course depends on how you define 'history'.

eds., *History and Imagination* (London, 1980), pp. 148–64; Charles Carlton, *Archbishop William Laud* (London, 1987), pp. 132–43; Kenneth Fincham, 'Early Stuart Polity', in Nicholas Tyacke, ed., *The History of the University of Oxford, Volume IV, Seventeenth-Century Oxford* (Oxford, 1997), pp. 179–210.

4 Colvin's conceptualization of post-medieval Gothic was typical of his generation – it was an aberration to be explained away – hence the title of his influential 'Gothic Survival and Gothic Revival', *Architectural Review*, CIII (March–June 1948), pp. 91–98 (reprinted in Howard Colvin, *Essays in English Architectural History* [New Haven and London, 1999], pp. 217–44). In 1983 he was still referring to Oxford's 'Retarded Renaissance' (*Unbuilt Oxford* [New Haven and London, 1983], p. 7). But by 1988 a certain post-modernity is discernible (*The Canterbury Quadrangle*, pp. 15–19).

For art historians such as myself, there is always a tendency to conceive history – 'real history' – not as an academic discipline but as 'everything else'. But I doubt if that is quite how V. H. Galbraith (1889–1976) or Austin Lane Poole (1889–1963) saw it. Galbraith was Regius Professor of Modern History at Oxford from 1948, while Lane Poole was President of St John's from 1947, and it was they, both senior medievalists, who engineered Colvin's move to Oxford in 1948, where he was to stay for the rest of his career.[5] Galbraith and Lane Poole wrote a kind of history that was primarily concerned with the publication of primary sources and the development of institutions (*The History of the King's Works* surely owes much to this tradition). In reality, then, the discipline of 'history' has always been prefaced by adjectives, albeit silent ones. Mid-twentieth-century history, moreover, scrupulously respected disciplinary boundaries. Thus *The White Canons in England*, Colvin's first book, excludes all discussion of Premon- stratensian architecture.[6]

There was, however, a connection between Colvin's work as a medieval historian and his subsequent emergence as an architectural historian. As David Watkin stated in *The Rise of Architectural History*, Colvin 'applied the techniques familiar in the study of medieval history to the study of post-mediaeval architecture, and thereby rendered architectural history academically respect-able.'[7] Colvin himself, recalling the 1930s in the mid-1990s, wrote that 'the factual basis of English architectural history was hopelessly amateurish', conclud-ing 'that the way to remedy the deficiency was to apply to architecture the ordinary processes of historical scholarship'.[8]

For Colvin, then, the interface between history and architectural history lay in documentation – in other words, not in *what* he said about buildings, but in *how* he went about researching them – and his greatness as a scholar lay in his capacity to locate archival sources and in the forensic rigour with which he interpreted them. From first to last, the archive lay at the heart of his work, and it was to the archive that he assigned the highest authority. Hence the following statement in *The Canterbury Quadrangle* (and countless others like it in other publications): 'in the absence of any scrap of documentation, Gerbier's possible involvement in the design of the Canterbury Quadrangle must remain an unsubstantiated hypothesis until some further piece of evidence, documentary or art-historical, is found, either to confirm or disprove it' (p. 52). The recourse 'art-historical' evidence was less characteristic.

[5] J. Mordaunt Crook, 'Howard Montagu Colvin, 1919–2007', *Proceedings of the British Academy*, CLXVI (2010); William Whyte, 'Colvin, Sir Howard Montagu (1919–2007)', *Oxford Dictionary of National Biography*.

[6] H. M. Colvin, *The White Canons in England* (Oxford, 1951).

[7] David Watkin, *The Rise of Architectural History* (London, 1980), p. 161.

[8] Colvin, *Essays in English Architectural History*, p. 292.

In other respects, however, Colvin's architectural history is not especially historical. He was always more interested in information than interpretation, in phenomena over causality. Colvin may have brought the archival rigour of medieval history to the interwar study of architecture (though we should not universalise the amateurism of the latter; Colvin himself acknowledged the exacting standards of the early *Survey of the London* volumes). But he never quite folded architecture into history, by which I mean he never sought to open up the range of sources at the historian's disposal. To say this is of course to flatten out the historiography of the twentieth century. The development of 'material culture' lay in the future, and as Colvin justifiably claimed in 1999 the biographical approach to British architecture was 'one fairly basic to its study in the state of knowledge prevailing in the 1950s'.[9] But his influence, as we shall see, was long lived.

There were of course exceptions, most notably *Architecture and the After-Life*, his history of western funerary architecture, which he published with Yale University Press in 1991. Written in retirement, this substantial book constituted a striking departure for Colvin, not only in its vast chronological and geographic range – from megalithic Sardinia to late-Victorian Farnborough – but for the way he set aside his usual engagement with documentation and wrote directly from the buildings. The result is both an architectural history of mausolea and a cultural history of burial. Two reasons for this methodological shift suggest themselves. Firstly, the principal themes of *Architecture and the After-Life* – commemoration and intercession – hark back to *The White Canons*, thereby facilitating a meaningful synthesis of history and architecture. And secondly, funerary monuments have always been a defining concern of English antiquarianism, and Colvin undoubtedly sat within this tradition. But *Architecture and the After-Life* is nevertheless exceptional, and the remainder of his career was given over, in the main, to the third (1995) and fourth (2008) editions of the *Biographical Dictionary* – back to archive-based enquiry, aimed at solving questions of when and by whom.

* * *

I have focussed on Colvin's *Canterbury Quadrangle* because the relationship between architecture and history seems to me most relevant to the current state of post-medieval British architectural history. Broadly speaking, there are two kinds of work currently being written, both of which configure the relationship between architecture and history in different ways. For convenience sake, we might term these traditions 'the history of architecture' and 'architectural history'. The first of these – 'the history of architecture' – prioritises the archival record and

[9] Colvin, *Essays in English Architectural History*, p. 297.

traces the primary sources through to the finished building. It is the kind of writing we most readily associate with Colvin, and it has been the dominant mode of scholarship in this country for over half a century. The second kind of writing – 'architectural history' – pays less attention to the archival record, and prefers to see the building itself as the document. This latter kind of writing is less concerned with the provision of new information and more interested in issues of interpretation.

These two trends are not mutually exclusive, but they have tended to fracture in recent years, to the detriment of both. Both traditions, moreover, have their methodological problems, and it is these limitations, I would now like to argue, that are thwarting the development of the discipline. Let's begin with the problems, as they point the way to how these traditions might be fruitfully combined.

The 'history of architecture' continues to be executed to the highest standards, in large part because of the exacting standards set by Colvin. We should recognise that our knowledge of the primary sources is formidable, and that the factual basis of British architectural history is probably unrivalled in Europe; we are *good* at the archive. But we should also acknowledge that our focus remains narrow. The questions we ask of the archive still predominantly pertain to dating and authorship, and few people outside a small circle of practitioners take much notice or care very much.

Should we blame Colvin for this? It was undoubtedly he, for the reasons discussed above, who initiated this tradition of scholarship, but in his defence we might say two things. Firstly, the *Biographical Dictionary* was always intended by its author as a means to an end, and secondly, like all pioneers, Colvin quickly attracted followers. The emphasis he placed on documentation, and the questions he asked of these sources, therefore became the dominant mode of the scholarly community *en tout*. Colvin's followers and admirers (myself included) have added our penny's worth to that growing pile of 'ascertainable fact'. And on it grows, something admirable and unique. But in doing so we have neglected to ask other questions of the archive.

In recent decades, however, a second strand of scholarship has risen to the fore – what I call 'architectural history'. Broadly speaking, this kind of work endeavours to relate architectural form to broader historical phenomena. The building becomes the historian's means, not his ends. The kind of writing I am describing is not the social history of architecture. Mark Girouard set the gold standard here, and others have followed suit, most notably Simon Thurley in his work on the royal palaces. The kind of scholarship I have in mind is less concerned with how society functioned within buildings, than with how architecture functioned within society – in short, it is the cultural history of architecture. Such work has reconfigured the relationship between architecture and history as the relationship between architecture and culture, and in so doing makes a presumption about the extent to which architectural meaning resonated across society. But the 'architectural history' project, if it can be described as such, is struggling to recover these meanings, in my view for two interrelated reasons. The first is a problem of methodology, while the second problem is a void in our knowledge. I say this not as someone opposed to this kind of writing, but as someone trying to work out how to do it well, as a practitioner and an educator.

The first of these problems is ultimately an error of category. It relates to the issue of not *what* architecture means, but *how* it does so. Faced with the difficulty of relating artefacts to culture, much of the recent scholarship, whether consciously or not, has equated architectural meaning with the operation of language. The analogy between architecture and language is of course an ancient one,[10] usually prompted by architecture's 'tendency to govern itself by rules, rules for the combination and distribution of architectural parts', which 'seems ... to display a kind of 'syntax'.'[11] John Summerson's *Classical Language of Architecture* is the classic example of this analogy worked through.[12] Semantic interpretations of architecture, however, go beyond ideas of syntax, and make claims not about form *per se*, but about its capacity to signify in ways akin to language. This presumption has become a commonplace, and it ultimately explains why bookshops are currently full of books such as *How to read a country house*, or *How to read a parish church*, books which in former decades would have contained a different verb in their title (*How to look at ...*). But the trend is likewise apparent in academic writing. The most recent book on Sir John Vanbrugh, for example, is subtitled *Storyteller in Stone*.[13]

This is of course symptomatic of a wider trend in the humanities: the tendency to regard all cultural phenomona as 'text'. If objects meant things within specific cultures, the structuralist argument runs, then these meanings are there to be 'read'. In saying this, however, the notions of 'text' and 'reading' are being extended beyond their literal selves – 'text' and 'reading' become metaphors for the ubiquity and instantiation of meaning; they represent an extension of the

[10] The literature on this subject is vast. For excellent introductions to it, see Georgia Clarke and Paul Crossley, eds, *Architecture and Language: constructing identity in European architecture c. 1000–c. 1650* (Cambridge, 2000); William Whyte, 'How Do Buildings Mean? Some issues of interpretation in the history of architecture', *History and Theory*, 45 (2006), pp. 153–77.

[11] Roger Scruton, *The Aesthetics of Architecture* (London, 1979), p. 160.

[12] John Summerson, *The Classical Language of Architecture* (London, 1996).

[13] Vaughan Hart, *Sir John Vanbrugh: storyteller in stone* (New Haven and London, 2008). See my review in the *Journal of the Society of Architectural Historians* 69 (2010), pp. 276–77. The ensuing paragraphs are an extension of the criticism I offer there.

literal into the realm of the visual. It is not my intention to refute architectural meaning. But when we take metaphors literally we kill them, for we destroy the subtle balance of equivalence that they contain within themselves. The truth of this particular metaphor is that architecture, like language, is capable of signifying things. *But it does so differently.*

In language, meaning is effected through a relationship between words (signifiers) and reality (signified). (The more radical claims of linguistic theory – that language determines the categories it describes – have had no impact on British architectural history.) Where language is concerned, this relationship is a very particular one, for two interrelated reasons. Firstly, the relationship between the signifier and the thing it signifies is arbitrary, since there is no intrinsic relationship between the two, at least not ordinarily (onomatopoeia is the well-known exception). And secondly, linguistic meaning tends to precision. Take the word 'column'. What, if anything, is columnar about it? Nothing, for it bears no resemblance to the thing it describes. The meaning of the word is rooted in convention, and it is this convention that distinguishes its meaning from that of other words, words such as 'entablature' or 'pediment'. The efficacy of language depends on precision.

But architectural meaning is not like this, for it is seldom arbitrary, and it is almost never precise; as Roger Scruton states, 'if it were true that architecture were a language (or, perhaps, a series of languages), then we should know how to understand every building, and the human significance of architecture would no longer be in question.'[14] We have just seen how words, in the main, are arbitrary signs, with no purpose beyond their capacity to signify. They are mere labels. But this is not true of buildings, which exist in their own right, prior to any signification they might assume. Thus, if architecture conveys meaning, it does so by recourse to an existing reality. So let's return to our column, not as a word this time, but as an architectural member, existing in reality. If we allow the column to become the signifier rather than the signified, what, we must then ask, does *it* mean? Our first response, if we are honest, will probably be bafflement, for architectural meaning is never precise or obvious. But if we continue to contemplate our column, we find that its range of possible meanings are ultimately provoked by the thing itself and the role it performs in the architectonics of building. In other words, its meaning is provoked by its nature and purpose, like a smile on a face. A more accurate metaphor than language would therefore be metaphor itself, for like metaphor, architectural meaning involves the transference of architecture's essential nature to other things. These

[14] Scruton, *Aesthetics of Architecture*, p. 158.

other things are not architecture, but the comparison with architecture helps us to comprehend them.

The presumption that architectural meaning operates like language is therefore a false one, and structuralist readings that perpetuate this fallacy are prone to certain pitfalls. I would like to outline three of these pitfalls.

I have already touched upon the first and most important of these: a blindness to the fused relationship between form and meaning. If the signifier is arbitrary, why dwell on it for more than a moment? We therefore prioritise signification over the signifier (meaning over form), and move immediately from form to meaning. This has two consequences. Firstly, we overlook the extent to which the form itself activates the meaning. We therefore denature architectural meaning. The second consequence is an exaggerated recourse to other things. For if we deny that architectural meaning depends on the signifier (on form), we are forced to go in search of these meanings elsewhere. Architectural meaning is severed from itself and becomes dependent on things that are, at worst, merely analogous, such as heraldry, literary technique, or the body. Heraldry is often resorted to in structuralist interpretations of architecture, since heraldry, unlike architecture, *is* a mode of visual signification in which signs are precise and (in the main) arbitrary, and, as such, is genuinely akin to language. Heraldry therefore conceals the disparity between architecture and language.

But what of architectural theory? Here, surely, is a body of precise meanings, widely understood at specific moments in history. Vitruvius, after all, allows us to see the column as male, female, and everything in between. He also allows us to see columns in relation to nature, via the column's elemental prototype, the tree trunk. Yes, these meanings pre-exist, and are therefore, like language, things that can be learnt and absorbed into convention. These meanings, however, depend ultimately on the poetics of architectural form, since they are metaphors provoked by the varying proportions and contrasting ornaments of the orders.

My second pitfall is the exaggerated emphasis placed on the small-scale unit, since, in interpretations of this kind, individual forms are made to carry the function of 'words'. The choice of orders, for example, becomes the basis for implausible flights of interpretation.[15]

My final pitfall is the presumption that meaning resides on the surface. This has at least two consequences. Firstly, it privileges the exteriors of buildings over their interiors, which is surely – to perpetuate the literary analogy for argument's sake – to judge a book by its cover. And secondly, it severs the building from its sources. If meaning resides in the object itself, why bother to trace its prehistory through the sources? William Whyte has rightly warned against this superficiality.

[15] Vaughan Hart, *Inigo Jones: the architect of kings* (New Haven and London, 2011).

Meaning, he persuasively argues, can (and should) be recovered from every stage of a building's life.[16]

This brings me to my second principal point. Both of these traditions of scholarship, owing to their methodological limitations, have overlooked an important body of material. This is the void I alluded to above, and it is *an understanding of how architecture was conceptualised in the past*. The void is due on the one hand to the limited enquiry of the 'history of architecture', and on the other to the presumption of 'architectural history' that architectural meaning is to be recovered by recourse to other things.

By identifying this shared blind spot, we arrive at the solution of how to write a more sophisticated architectural history. The remedy, I believe, is to unite the two scholarly approaches I have described above. By extending the questions we ask of the archive, we can begin to understand how architecture was understood in early modern England. A broadening of the first tradition will provide a remedy for the second.

The first step, then, is to recover how architecture was understood in the period itself. In short, we need to construct an intellectual history of our medium. I use the term 'intellectual history' in the broadest sense, to suggest a systematic exposition – and it would need to be Colvinesque in scale – of the various ways in which every sector of society conceptualised architecture and building at this time. This would need to encompass much more than architectural publications – which have of course been magnificently studied by Eileen Harris and Nick Savage[17] – and look at letters, poems, journals, newspapers, and just about any other source that sheds light on how people thought about architecture. The ubiquity of architectural metaphor also needs to be systematically studied. This is a project of no less magnitude than that facing Colvin in the immediate post-war period, and I predict that it will dominate our discipline in the decades ahead.

Only once we have recovered these ideas of architecture will we begin to understand how architecture signified in English culture. In short, we cannot write a cultural history of architecture until we have understood its intellectual history. At present, we struggle to understand what people were doing with buildings because we do not understand what they thought buildings were. By grounding architectural meaning in the study of *architecture*, a truer understanding of its meanings will follow.

* * *

In the final part of this paper, then, I would like to return briefly to the Canterbury

16 Whyte, 'How Do Buildings Mean?'.

17 Eileen Harris and Nicholas Savage, *British Architectural Books and Writers, 1556–1785* (Cambridge, 1990).

Quadrangle – the building now, not the book – and ask what, if anything, did its architecture mean to Caroline Oxford? I do so via the method advocated above, and to that end turn to Laud himself. How did he conceptualise architecture?

We turn, then, to his complete works, which run to nine worthy volumes.[18] Architecture, it must be admitted, does not figure prominently in them. When he mentions it at all, he does so fleetingly, usually in sermons and letters. But this should not surprise us, for architecture was not a priority; and it is precisely because he mentions architecture obliquely that he reveals so much about his underlying thinking on the subject. There is enough, however, to demonstrate that he thought about architecture in two principal ways.

Firstly, and very naturally, he equated buildings with institutions. It would be impossible to exaggerate the importance that institutions held for Laud, and the depth of emotion that they provoked in him. He lived his life in them, through them, and for them; and when his career descended into humiliation and chaos, the nightmare he dreamed was the architectural ruination of the institution he loved best, St John's.[19] This fervour was partly driven by his socio-political vision, which, as we have already seen, equated institutions with authority, and it was this vision that informed his stewardship of the college, the university, and the kingdoms as a whole. But what of their architecture? In Laud's mind, buildings not only accommodated institutions; they proclaimed their dignity. This was to be effected through decorum, and for Laud appropriateness was realized not by recourse to Vitruvian theory but by conformity to medieval typologies. Experiencing Protestantism in the raw on a visit to Scotland, he complained that the galleried interior of St Giles's Cathedral in Edinburgh looked

> for all the world like a square theatre, without any show of a church; as is also the Church at Brunt Island ... I remember, when I passed over at the Frith, I took it at first sight for a large square pigeon-house; so free was it from all suspicion of being so much as built like an ancient church.[20]

For Laud, then, a church had to look like a church. And in order for a church to look like a church, it had to look like those that came before it. This is not just a question of architecture resembling itself, but of it doing so within a wider architectural inheritance. Such an attitude, by no means unique to Laud, was subsequently given theoretical formulation by Sir Christopher Wren, who characterized it as 'customary beauty'.[21]

18 *The Works of the Most Reverend Father in God William Laud* (7 vols.; Oxford, 1847–60).

19 Laud, *Works*, III, p. 246.

20 Laud, *Works*, III, p. 315.

21 Anthony Geraghty, *The Sheldonian Theatre: architecture and learning in seventeenth-century Oxford* (New Haven and London, 2013), pp. 43–46.

The second way that architecture features in Laud's writings is as metaphor. In this instance the architecture is explicitly classical, and deployed to convey ideas of status, power, and hierarchy. In so doing, he makes no mention of actual buildings, and the architecture he evokes is purely conceptual. Here is a telling example, from a letter of March 1639 (or thereabouts) to the Earl of Strafford, describing Laud's newly marginalized position at court. Continuing an architectural metaphor that had evidently been introduced by Strafford, Laud writes:

> Tis true ... these are the great stars in the firmament. But you had rather metaphorize them in architecture, and place your rustic pillars below where you please, and these Corinthian eminent. You brag of Vitruvius, and yet talk of the standing of these pillars set upon pinnacles. Good Vitruvius, remember yourself – when did you find any Corinthian pillars set upon pinnacles? And yet you cannot hold from boasting that I should take heed how I provoke you in the phrase of architecture.[22]

The precise meaning of all this is unclear, as only one half of the correspondence survives. But Strafford had evidently likened his fallen position at court to that of a 'rustic pillar', contrasting this with those newly in the ascendant – the 'Corinthian eminence'. In so doing, he acknowledges the traditional hierarchy of the orders, but like others he struggled with the precise nature of architectural language ('the phrase of architecture'), confusing 'pinnacles' for (one assumes) pedestals, hence Laud's affectionate rebuke. In his reply, Laud does not extend the analogy, but he does make claim to a superior knowledge of classical architecture and to its textual basis in Vitruvius. It is the learned nature of this correspondence that is most revealing. Classical architecture has become an intellectual accomplishment, and, as such, a sophisticated way of describing the real subject of the letter: politics. It is no coincidence that he writes thus to Strafford – a fellow courtier – and his letters to the same contain other allusions to high culture, all deployed allegorically: to the draftsmanship of Van Dyck and the poetry of Donne, which he labels not metaphysical but anagrammatic.[23] Both men are clearly conforming to some kind of elite conduct. Laud, however, does so teasingly, gently mocking Strafford's claim of aesthetic sophistication.

Architecture as institution and architecture as intellectual accomplishment. This same duality appears in the sculpted decoration of the Canterbury Quadrangle. On the west side, the spandrels of the arcade are decorated with personifications of the seven virtues. As there were eight roundels to fill, Religion was added, identified by bibles and churches. Once again, then, we find the institution of the church equated with her buildings, and we see her buildings

[22] Laud, *Works*, VII, p. 538
[23] Laud, *Works*, VI, pp. 523–24; VII, p. 295

Fig. 4. 2. Religion, The Canterbury Quadrangle, St John's College, Oxford

given form by reference to medieval precedent, hence the crenellated towers, cusped lancets, and pastry-like window tracery (Fig. 4.2). The spandrels on the other side of the Quadrangle are decorated with the seven liberal arts. Architecture again makes an appearance (Fig. 4.3), but this time not in the guise of a building but as a book: as Vitruvius. This, together with Euclid, Archimedes and Hypsicles, identifies Geometry, a reminder that architecture, though never taught in the Oxford schools, was nevertheless conceptualized as a mathematical science and thus nominally a part of learning.

Thus we see Gothic architecture as a building and equated with an institution, and classical architecture as a book and equated with learning. Can we extend this duality to the building itself? To a degree, I think we can. As is well known, the Canterbury Quadrangle is composed of two architectural styles or traditions, combining, as it does, many of the traditional features of collegiate design with – as Colvin so scrupulously demonstrated – a Continental mode of classicism and ornament (Fig. 4.4). These two modes, however, are carefully

Fig. 4. 3. Geometry, The Canterbury Quadrangle, St John's College, Oxford

distinguished from one another; this is not, as is often claimed, hybrid architecture. Classicism is carefully limited (on the exterior of the building) to the principal doorways, the frontispieces, and the two arcades.

It is the Gothic parts of the building (some of which, it must be admitted, pre-existed) that affirm the Quadrangle's institutional heritage. The windows are consistently of the standard two-arched type, characteristic of collegiate architecture since the fifteenth century (although without cusping), and the quadrangle as a whole is tied together by the upper string course, with its emphatically-scaled grotesques, and by the battlements that terminate the facades. These features associate the project with the norms of college design. More specifically, the fan-vaulted passageways leading to and from the quadrangle were surely conceived with reference to the great episcopal foundations of New College, All Souls, and Magdalen, where elaborate vaults are similarly located. The quadrangle perpetuates the typology of the Oxford college, and thereby emphasizes Laud's perpetuation of episcopal patronage within the university. The form of the

Fig. 4. 4. The Canterbury Quadrangle, from David Loggan, *Oxonia illustrata* (1675), detail.

building advertises Laud as successor to Wykeham, Waynflete, Chichele, and Wolsey.

The classical elements at St John's, however, stand outside this medieval inheritance. I feel certain these are not meant to be representational in any pictorial sense, in the way that the medieval elements of the quadrangle are: they are not intended to evoke preexisting buildings or typologies. How, then, are we to make sense of them? Let's begin with the classical doorways, the meaning of which becomes apparent when we think about them in relation to their function within the wider ensemble. Their purpose is simple: they denote the principal entrances to and from the Quadrangle and thereby articulate its hierarchy of spaces (this is likewise true of the elaborate doorways within the library). The frontispieces are an extension of this, their purpose being firstly to denote the principal axis through the college and secondly (like their less developed counterparts at Merton, Wadham, and the Schools Quadrangle) to frame information (heraldic and sculptural) about the building's wider origins, purpose, and status. Rather than contribute to the typology of the building, I would suggest they offer a commentary upon it. As in Laud's letter to Strafford, they are deployed metaphorically, to express associations of rank and hierarchy; Charles and Maria take centre stage as the 'Corinthian eminent'. The purpose of the frontispieces is best understood by reference to their bibliographic namesakes: frontispieces to books, which likewise epitomize the contents of the book to which they are attached.[24] And like a printed frontispiece, the orders are not only framing this information but contributing to its import. An architectural frontispiece cannot rely on the distinction between word and image, but an equivalent distinction is effected at St John's by the knowing juxtaposition of architectural style.

It can be demonstrated, then, that the architectural forms of the Canterbury Quadrangle are consistent with the principal ways that Laud conceptualized architecture. By recovering these ideas, we can begin to understand what Laud intended his building to signal, and the extent to which architectural form was marshaled to these ends. We see a building that proclaims its place within the longer architectural and patronal traditions of the university, and that asserts the loyalty of the university, and of Laud personally, to the higher institution of monarchy. Not everyone would have recognized it as such, but until we begin to recover the wider culture of early modern architecture we will be, as Laud might have said, building without foundations.

[24] They are referred to as 'fronts' in the accounts (Colvin, *Canterbury Quadrangle*, p. 33). Christy Anderson has referred to a 'frontispiece mentality' in early modern England (*Inigo Jones and the Classical Tradition* [Cambridge, 2007], p. 153).

Chapter Five

THE CONUNDRUM OF 'BY'

Andrew Saint

What a hunger for biographical dictionaries there seems to be nowadays. In the domain of architecture Howard Colvin bears the palm. The first edition of his *Biographical Dictionary* – confined to England – came out in 1954. The second followed in 1976, the third, extended to Wales and Scotland, in 1995, the fourth in 2008. On that quickening pace a fifth will be due around 2018. The appetite for fresh versions of 'Colvin' seems inexhaustible.

In recent years he has had disciples, or competitors. Under the late Sir Alec Skempton there appeared in 2002 the invaluable *Biographical Dictionary of Civil Engineers, Volume I*, covering the years 1500 to 1830, a work which seems to have learnt everything from Colvin except perfectionism of indexing. The follow-up for 1830 to 1890 under Cross-Rudkin and Chrimes came out in 2008, and the 'Civils' are now at full tilt on Volume Three. To these may be added Rolf Loeber's *Biographical Dictionary of Architects in Ireland, 1600–1720* (1981), again exactly on the Colvin model; John Harvey's *English Mediaeval Architects* (1954, revised edn. 1984, supplement 1987) proving in his view that it was nonsense of William Morris to claim that there were not any; and Sarah Bendall's *Dictionary of Land Surveyors* (1997), going up to 1850. Not quite the same, yet bearing the imprint of Colvin's pervasive organizing influence, is *British Architectural Books and Their Writers 1556–1785* (1990) by Eileen Harris with Nicholas Savage.

All of these are just printed books. If we supplement them with what is available on line, we have to add David Walker's exemplary *Dictionary of Scottish Architects 1840–1980*, wider in scope than it sounds and continually expanding; and more recently Ann Martha Rowan's *Dictionary of Irish Architects 1720–1940* on a similar model. Both these latter ventures pick up from the date where the books before them stopped. By virtue of their flexibility and interrogability they also suggest we shall see few further printed books of this kind in future.

Can any country outside the British Isles boast a comparable line-up of up-to-date biographical dictionaries for the built environment? We can be proud of all the scholarship that has followed in Colvin's wake and largely on his model. Nor does it stop at buildings. 2009 saw the appearance of the *Biographical Dictionary of Sculptors in Britain, 1660–1851*, alias the 'New Gunnis', published like the later editions of Colvin by Yale University Press with a subsidy from the ever-bountiful Paul Mellon Centre. The original edition of the *Dictionary of British Sculptors* indeed pipped Colvin to the post by a year, coming out in 1953. But Rupert Gunnis did not live to revise his monument, as Colvin did, not once, not twice, but thrice and in full.

Recently, the horticultural scholar Brent Elliott wrote a piece for the London Library's in-house magazine about that institution's collection of biographical dictionaries.[1] International in scope, his article drew attention to all manner of exotic and handy treasures, from the *Almanac de Gotha* to the portentous *Dizioniario Biografico degli Italiani*, which after 73 volumes and 51 years has reached the letter M. Compare that to the revised *Oxford Dictionary of National Biography*: 60 volumes in 12 years; available on line, though alas not free; in continuous revision, yet still retaining a residuum of the best articles and jokes from Leslie Stephen's Victorian original. Those who have occasion to seek out obscurer biographical information from French or German or even American sources, whether on architects or others, will know that the same wealth of resource is not so readily available elsewhere.

There can be little doubt that biography is a British addiction. Seldom a year goes by without some smug article in the review section of one of the higher-brow papers proclaiming ours to be a golden age and place for biography, whatever we may feel has happened to the novel, and customarily alluding to Michael Holroyd and the Bloomsbury Group. I wonder whether all this is so new, and whether the inflated Victorian commemorations of statesmen and prelates, replete with their earnest correspondence, were not also rarer on the Continent. Some of the more gossipy biographical obsessions of the English certainly puzzle our neighbours. Can it really matter, they sometimes ask, who Lytton Strachey slept with, which wealthy lady owned which of the houses where Raine Maria Rilke immured himself to try and complete the *Duino Elegies*, or whether Cézanne loved his mother more than his wife? Surely what matters are the books and poems they wrote, the pictures they painted. The rest is irrelevant.

The broad answer to that is easy to give, even if many examples of prurience and tittle-tattle are indefensible on any higher grounds than the malicious pleasures of gossip. We are interested in how people live – not just artists, writers and architects – because it sheds light upon what they do, and vice versa. In our own case of architectural scholarship, humanity is vital if it is not to be mere archaeology. Bricks and mortar can be dull and dry things. We want to know as much as we can about the people who bring them together, shape them, and make them bold or beautiful, and how. We also want to know about the men and

1 *London Library Magazine*, Spring 2011, pp. 22–4.

women who cause and pay these people to do that making and shaping, who live in and adapt the results, and again how. The buildings illuminate the people, and the people the buildings. That is what architectural biography in the broadest of senses does, or ought to do, and what the longer entries in Colvin's dictionary consistently achieve.

There is no commoner beginning to the study of architecture than to be drawn in by biographical curiosity. Students besotted by the personalities of Le Corbusier or Mackintosh still apply to schools of architecture. Often scholars too start with an individual career, before delving deeper. Biography is not only human, it is a natural introductory and organizing principle in any field of historical study. Tracing someone's career, particularly after about 1700 when there is usually enough information to do so, gives shape to the subject's age and circumstances and styles, and allows one to watch patterns of practice and culture unfold around their evolving lives. Just as a section unlocks and explains a building, so at its best the biographical study offers a framework, a discipline and a penetration which together can unlock and explain events.

All that works best for the bigger players, about whom more is known or can be dug out, and who intersect ambitiously and successfully with their times. But what about the low- to middle-ranking figures who occupy most of Colvin's pages and indeed are often the topic nowadays of monographic articles or even books? They seldom tell us so much about the spirit of their particular age, nor do their buildings require undue illumination or interpretation. In many if not most such studies, notably the dictionaries mentioned at the start, enlightenment via biography takes second place to something different.

A brutal way of describing this might be train-spotting; or, if you prefer it, stamp-collecting. A lot of British architectural history nowadays seems to be all about these two very English (and very male) hobbies. Why? What do we learn from it? And can it go on?

Train-spotting and stamp-collecting belong to a genre of innocent, instinctive activities or games which go back to childhood and which for perfectly amiable reasons many of us never quite abandon. They can certainly help to refresh the drudgery of scholarship. Here are a few examples from my recent experience.

At *The Survey of London* we have been busy recently in Battersea. Here there once were a fair number of villas round the fringes of Clapham Common, built for City merchants between about 1760 and 1840 – perfect Colvin territory. Only a few survive, and for those that do as well as those that do not, we seldom have the name of an architect. This itches: that is the best description I can give. All the time we are hoping that a deed or an account will turn up the name. On the rare occasions when it does, or when we can confidently make an attribution, as in the case of one famous house, Battersea Rise, which we are pretty sure was designed

Fig. 5.1. Battersea Rise, the front. Designed for Isaac Ackerman around 1760, probably by Robert Taylor. Later the home of Henry Thornton and William Wilberforce. Demolished in 1908.
English Heritage, London Region

by Robert Taylor (Fig. 5.1), there is rejoicing in the office. We then feel we can write something in the margin of our interleaved copy of Colvin, using the dictionary rather like one of Ian Allan's old trainspotters' guides.

This sleuthing can work the other way round too. Look up David Laing in Colvin, and you find an entry which reads: 'Lavender Hill, Wandsworth, Surrey, villa "erected" before 1818, probably for Ephraim Gompertz [Plans, pl 42]'. The reference takes one to a book of designs issued by Laing in 1818, illustrating a small, plain villa (Fig. 5.2). There is nothing to identify precisely where it was built, except that the text in the book of designs states it was west-facing. My colleague Philip Temple then scours the large-scale Ordnance map to find a west-facing villa of the right size. Again, rejoicing when he finds that the only one

Villa, Lavender Hill, Surrey.

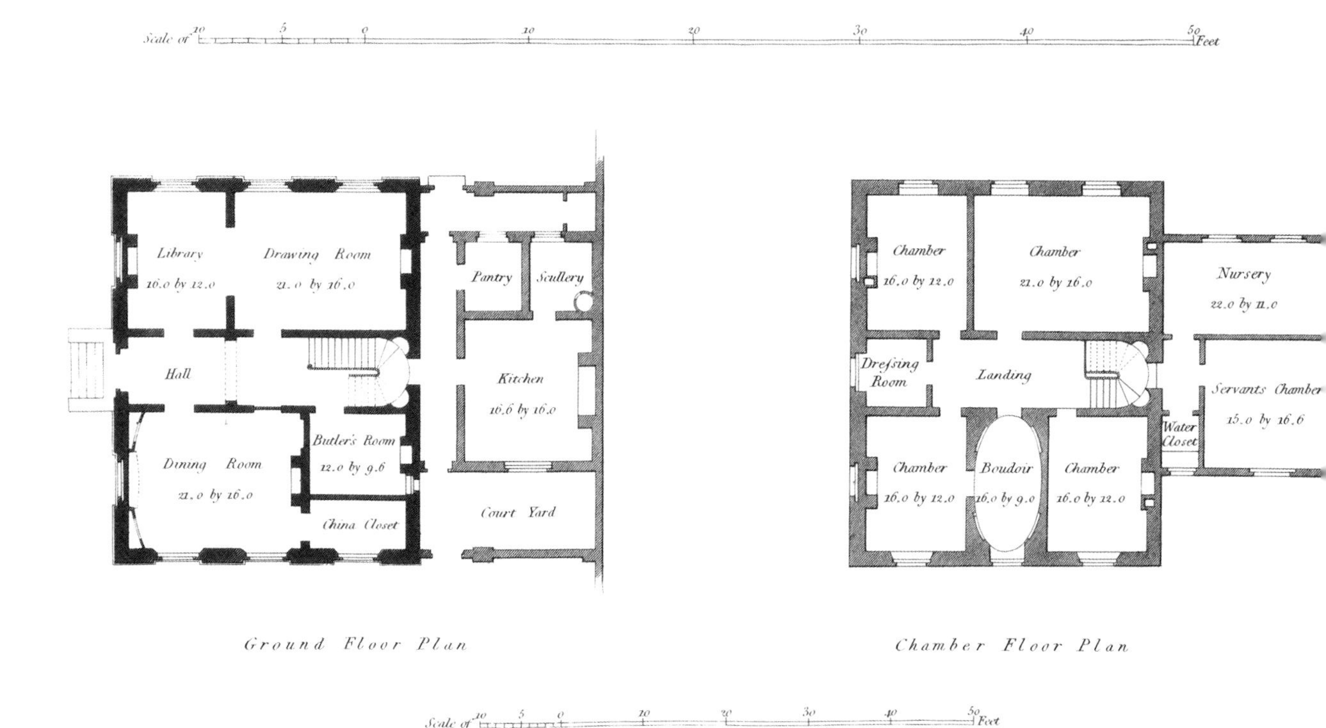

Fig. 5.2. The Chesnuts, Lavender Hill. Elevation and plans of villa for Ephraim Gomperz as published by David Laing, 1818.

Fig. 5.3. The Chesnuts, Lavender Hill, in 1972, encumbered by late Victorian housing in Mossbury Road, Clapham Junction. *English Heritage, London Region*

that fits still exists, though blisteringly altered and encumbered by later housing (Fig. 5.3). So Volume 50 of *The Survey of London* will reveal to a grateful world that The Chesnuts, Clapham Junction, is by David Laing. Meanwhile our interleaved Colvin has been further annotated.

One last case. Anyone who has done time teasing out the truth about how the fabric of any British city got built up will know that there is a boundless supply of humble architects and surveyors eager to step out from the shadows and enjoy their brief moment in the beam of history. In any area of London one accumulates a parochial *oeuvre* by these men: in Battersea, for instance, Charles Lee, the Nash assistant, surveyor and speculator; the minor aesthetic designer Zephaniah King (Fig. 5.4); H. I. Newton, the rumbustious pub architect; Herbert Bignold, author of sundry suburban houses and flats plus a lavish bakery. There is a pleasure to be had just in collecting and categorizing these obscurities, as there is a pleasure in collecting anything. But because they are human beings, it runs deeper. Exhumation brings an almost mystical satisfaction, as dim figures climb out of the grave once more. It is good, too, to light up some humdrum streets with a glint of life. Human beings, one comes to realize, interest the typical *Survey of London* reader

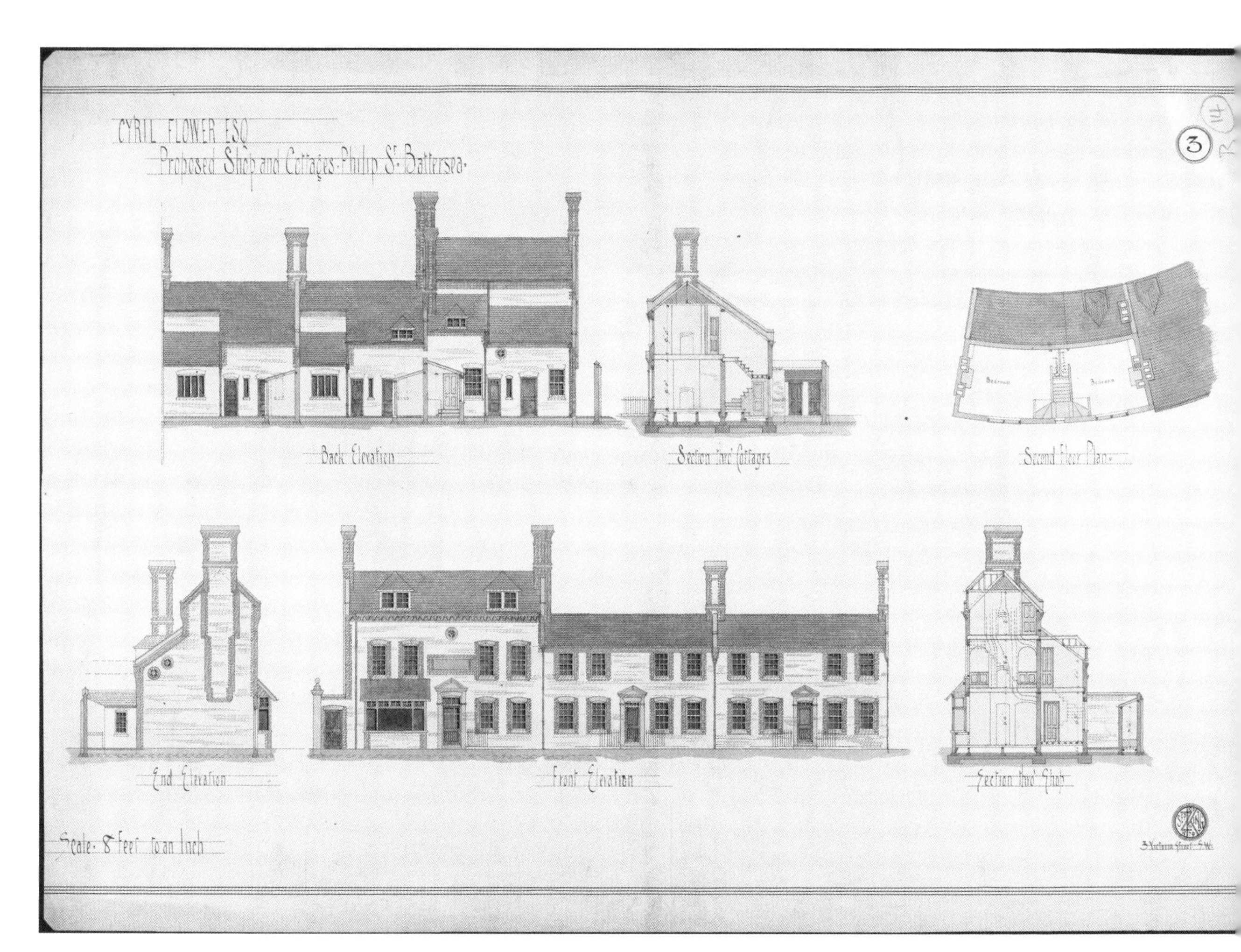

Fig. 5.4. St Philip Street, Park Town Estate, Battersea. Elevations, plans and sections of houses and shops by Zephaniah King, 1879, with the architect's aesthetic monogram in corner.
London Metropolitan Archive

more than bricks and mortar. (What one also comes to realize is that the human beings who interest readers most are not the people who created these streets but the people who inhabited them, above all those who were their ancestors.)

Whatever our reasons for wanting to record and perpetuate the names and lives of such humble designers and creators, they do not seem to have much to do with art. And here arises the conundrum of my title. Because the usual excuse given – when it is given, which is seldom – for all our train-spotting and stamp-collecting is that to document and identify the authorship of a building in some way illuminates a creative artist at work. Particularly in Britain, the job of the architectural historian is often assumed to be the earnest pursuit of that task of identification, *à la* Colvin, until every half-worthwhile building is accurately ascribed, documented and docketed.

That is the kind of rationale set out for art-historical biography in, for instance, George Kubler's *The Shape of Time* (1962). It seems to be the unstated basis of Colvin's motivations and methodology, taken for granted perhaps because it is very far from unique to him. This was cutting-edge stuff for Colvin's generation. It has been developed farthest and, as far as habits of thinking about approaches to British architecture go, most influentially in the *Pevsner Architectural Guides*. The first editions by Pevsner himself, when the series was still *The Buildings of England*, are most to the point, because most economical. The information they give is a shorthand, as Pevsner was well aware it had to be. If he did not have the space or knowledge to say more, he just said a building was 'by' some architect or other, with the date. Today we have forgotten how odd this would have looked to earlier enthusiasts and travellers, going about with their Little Guides and their Arthur Mees in hand. By the same token, it is likely to look odd to future generations.

Now Pevsner, as everyone has forcibly been reminded by dint of not one but two recent biographies, was an art historian, trained in the exacting German methodology of that discipline. Art history has always been dominated by the fine arts, often to its detriment. And what the word 'by' means in the fine arts is not only somewhat different from what it means in architecture, it also has different implications. In the simplest case, a gallery painting is painted by an individual, in other words designed and carried out from start to finish by the same person. The reality, we know, is often not so simple. Raphael, Rubens, and Reynolds all had pupils or shops; the great man may have done the sketch, but frequently did only a portion of the painting. The point of accurate ascriptions and catalogues in the field of painting is more than scholarly precision or pleasure or train-spotting. It is a practical science, because the degree of involvement of the master, if any, has a dramatic effect on sale value. Authentication means money.

There can certainly be occasions when attributions of buildings affect their value. Lutyens's houses, for example, are invariably advertised as such, and reportedly worth more on the market. Architects' names do indeed seem increasingly to feature in estate agents' particulars, but it is doubtful if they do more than add a fresh tang to the snobbishness that has always attached to these items. Whether a mansion is given in Colvin to Smith of Warwick or Carr of York will make little odds to its price. There is also the other side to that coin. A house by a smart architect will mean a listed house, where the owners will be restricted in what they can do. On that consideration, down rather than up will go the price. When however architectural drawings or architect-designed objects are in the frame, attribution certainly does make a difference. If someone asks an expert on a given architect whether a house is by that architect, it is likely to be for reasons of curiosity or pride. But if he or she is asked to authenticate a drawing or a piece of furniture, the question usually conceals an interest in its sale value. Here too the saleroom wags the tail of this business of 'by'.

So in the fine arts and the salerooms an urgency and a raw practicality underlie all the scholarship and connoisseurship. With buildings (need it be reaffirmed that architecture and architectural drawings are not the same?) the case is otherwise. Not only does 'by' matter less in practical terms, it also means something different. 'By', indeed, has a subtly different meaning in each of the arts. It is straightforward enough in the case of a poet or solo artist, less so for playwrights or composers or film directors or architects, in other words all those art-forms which require collaboration to bring the work to fruition. The word 'by', or the possessive noun, as in Milton's *Paradise Lost*, Beethoven's Ninth, Canova's *The Three Graces*, or Kurosawa's *Rashomon*, is conventionally employed as a shorthand to assert individual ownership through some sustained, creative act. But in each case something different is implied. Each art-form has its own conventions of credit and attribution, and even its own traditional disputes about how these are allotted. In the film world, for instance, *auteur* theory was about trying to shift creative credit from the producer to the director. In the world of music, the balance of credit shifts back and forth between composer and performer, depending on the genre.

The further we move from autonomous creativity, the more puzzling and often downright misleading the word 'by' becomes. Take architecture. Does Richard Rogers *make* the buildings that are attributed to him, as a painter or composer or novelist conventionally makes a work of art? No. Does he *design* them himself? Hardly so. So in what sense can a building be said to be 'by' Rogers? Or to take another case where the fiction is more openly acknowledged, the great architectural departments of the public sector, did Hubert Bennett design the Queen Elizabeth Hall, or Robert Matthew the Royal Festival Hall, or Lewis Womersley Park Hill at Sheffield? For the most part, they did not. But there was a convention in those departments that the chief architect signed the drawings, or that a stamp with his signature was used on all drawings and letters, in the same way that lawyers' letters always go out over the name of the firm. Often assistants who have worked in big architectural offices, private as well as public, will say, 'he hardly saw that scheme which went out in his name until it got to committee'.

Now all these are cases from the twentieth century or after. That is partly why, apart from the scale of the task, there are no Colvins for the modern era, and never could be on the same coherent principle. But let us not imagine that similar issues do not arise for buildings and architects of the Colvin era. James Burton, for example: in what sense are the buildings attributed to him 'by' him? Or even Wren. What do we mean by the Wren churches? The truth is that for many architectural figures, including exceptionally creative ones like Wren, 'by' is a catch-all preposition. It stands for an organizational principle rather than a statement about artistry, and one that calls for different unpacking and understanding in each case to work out what it means. From Colvin onwards scholars have been taking the Wren *oeuvre* to pieces for years now, removing St Mary Aldermary from it, arguing to and fro about the dates and authorship of pieces of St Paul's, and so on. Just what is proven by this painstaking process is hard to say. Beyond moving the stamps around from one page of the album to another, it at least ought to remind us that architecture is more like a highly organized collaborative business than a fine art. The designer never stands alone.

Another case in point is Lord Burlington. Joseph Rykwert once told me that he went to a lecture in which Rudolph Wittkower showed beyond the shadow of a doubt that Burlington really designed the buildings given to his name. Albert Richardson was in the chair, and at the end thanked the lecturer genially for all his learned documentation and analysis, then added, 'But of course we all know the buildings are really by Kent'. The anecdote was supposed to show the rank insouciance of the architect-connoisseur. Yet crediting buildings to Burlington or any of the other famous amateurs of his day, whether it is done through drawings, documentation or the eye is quite a narrowly conceived business. It may even mislead, if it is suggested that only one person at a time can be creative in the making of architecture, or that only some identifiable act of design is a token of creativity. The questions involved admit of no closed or simple answer. The best we can hope for is to explain how people operated and with whom.

The same goes for almost everyone who is in the Colvin dictionary and all those other dictionaries I cited at the start, be they top-ranking or bottom-ranking. Architecture in all ages is intensely collaborative, and we mislead our readers if we present it as a craft of pure, creative individualism. In the Colvin years we have to deal at the least with client, architect, and builder, all of whom may be more than one person. As time goes on, building procurement involves an increasingly complex chain of connections. An ambitious project today may go from the client to the project manager, then to the architect, next to the quantity surveyor and the structural engineer and now also the services engineer, then back to the architect and the quantity surveyor and the project manager again, who arranges the tenders. Then the builder and all the subcontractors come in, and the work gets under way. At the end of it all comes the user of the building, who very likely will not be the client.

How to make sense of all that? Most people who like architecture are preoccupied by appearances and styles. So they focus on the architect, who seems to be most responsible for setting the shape and the look of a building – the 'design' as it is called for short – and therefore seems like the key creative figure. But it is seldom that easy. Were the Abbé Suger and William of Wykeham just clients, just the men with the money? We know that they were much more than that, or at least they were presented at the time as more than that. That presentation was part of how the medieval world thought and functioned, so we ought to take it seriously. Taking medieval architecture in the round, it makes sense to ascribe to the so-called patrons with a good deal of the credit, if it is credit we are interested in. Once that is done, John Harvey's crusade to elevate the craftsmen-architects of the fifteenth century into modern design-professionals can look as lopsided as William Morris's insistence that they merely worked with their hands. Or to take a recent example, we know that for the past century and a half engineers have worked with architects on the same buildings, sometimes alongside them and sometimes with them, moderating their ideas on occasions or egging them on, as figures like Ove Arup and Frank Newby famously did.

Architects like to come top, and we historians usually place them so. Should we be encouraging that? Vanity is the besetting deadly sin of the architectural profession, and it seems to be getting worse. Architectural magazines these days are as full of pictures of architects as of the buildings themselves. That is a great change from a century ago, when few people had an idea what Lutyens or Perret or Otto Wagner looked like.

In building, as in other areas of constructive and collaborative human activity, every case and every set of circumstances is different, and should surely be scrutinized on its merits, without rigid, snobbish and often misleading demarcations. The more we know, the better chance we have of getting the credits right, or at least in the right order. Most speculative housing, for instance, seems since the nineteenth century to have been designed by young architectural assistants or surveyors working anonymously for builders, who are the people nearest to being in charge. Then there are structures like bridges. Here since about 1800 it has been natural for engineers to take the lead, with architects trailing behind, at first adding on the decorative bits, more recently setting the design concept which the engineers have then to go and make work, or 'styling' an existing engineering design, as with Foster and the Millennium Bridge or the Millau Viaduct. We should be resolute in not letting the media get away with the notion that these bridges are 'by' Foster, or even Fosters, when they are not. No doubt people want simplicity, not a long string of film credits, but it is surely our duty to ensure these things are got as right as they can be.

Even if we restrict ourselves to design, it does not take much knowledge of the architectural process to appreciate that there are many ways of designing. Accordingly, the meanings and values attached to the term differ. Soane's obsessive method of design, for instance, was completely different from Nash's improvisational approach. Philip Webb did it all himself, but Norman Shaw let his better assistants loose on details, elevations, and whole minor buildings. Does the individualism of Soane or Webb make them better architects than Nash or Shaw? It would be a narrow-minded view of what architecture encompasses to insist on that. One common pattern is for busy architects to choose at an early stage from alternative design concepts started by their assistants, and then decide which is to be worked up. Eero Saarinen worked like that, so sometimes did Lubetkin, and Norman Foster is said to do so too. Another pattern is for assistants to get so complete an understanding of their master's mind that they can work up what he means from a thumbnail sketch into a complete, elaborated design. That is how the great late buildings of H. H. Richardson were done, with the master lying mortally ill in bed with Bright's disease, turning out little sketches which his adept assistants turned into the finished designs. You would have thought that when Richardson died they could have carried on at the same level, but it did not work out like that. The posthumous buildings lack the spark and the authority.

Here perhaps lies the key. In the end, 'by' in architecture does not mean design. What it means is authority, decisiveness, and control. Wren is the architect of the Wren churches and Norman Foster is the controlling partner of Fosters not because they design everything, not even because they originate the concept, but because they are in charge. A corrective stroke across a drawing, a word, even a phone call, is enough to assert that control. Anyone who has worked in large organizations knows that the right kind of authority has to be exercised if they are to function creatively. Even the big public-sector offices were like this. The London County Council Architect's Department under W. E. Riley and Robert Matthew felt like a creative place; under Topham Forrest it did not. In this way important architects and other so-called design professionals are less like the artists they aspire to appear than like the chief executive officers of large businesses. They do not operate like starving geniuses in Parisian garrets.

What relevance does all this have to Colvin? As after a bereavement, I would like to suggest that it's time to 'move on'. A fifth edition of the *Dictionary* would be valuable to have, online if possible, alongside further online biographical resources. Let there always be room for the happy innocence of train-spotting and stamp-collecting. But if we want really to understand how buildings get made and what place they occupy in the history of their times, we need to insist on a more grown-up level of interpretation. Perhaps we can only do so now that Colvin and his disciples have completed their essentially Victorian, almost utopian, project of global cataloguing and inventorization.

Where we should move on to is harder to say. But I have an urgent sense of what we should avoid. That is the take-over of architectural history by academic preoccupations, and the promotion of an increasingly esoteric scholarly and theoretical agenda. Look for instance at what has happened to western literature. Its great writers have all been docketed and expounded, leaving little of these useful tasks to do. The study of literature has gone inwards, and is in danger of getting lost within the academy. If we are not vigilant, the same could too easily happen with architecture now that the Colvinesque and Pevsnerian cataloguing is all but complete.

Our history has got to find ways of going on being useful, as Colvin so certainly is, and curious, as he always was too. It has also to go on being about campaigning, about teaching, and – perhaps the best way of attracting support and attention – it must go on being about having fun. In all this we have one thing on our side which the fine-art crowd do not have, or not to the same degree. Most buildings, paradoxically, are more fragile than paintings. They stand out in the rain and decay; people want to pull them down or mash them about. We have got to go on fighting for the buildings we care about, because when they are demolished or mangled they are more truly 'a loss to the nation' than when a Titian or Salvator Rosa is snapped up by the Getty. And as part of that vigilant campaigning we must maintain the unique creative crossover between amateurs and architects and historians and conservation professionals.

In that loose jumble I would be the first to welcome the humanizing role of biography and the sense of possession, indeed passion, denoted by the word 'by'. It gives a unique insight into the balance of context, power and money with brain, eye and hand which goes to make buildings. In the same way that some of us as children loved trains and stamps, even as adults we still seem to need to collect those clay-footed people called heroes. Let hero-worship flourish, and let Howard Colvin by all means be a hero and a model for those who write architectural history. But let our biographical explorations be more perceptive and inclusive than they too often have been; let them be less art-historical and, as a result, let them be fairer. Above all let's ensure that our train-spotting and stamp-collecting do not stand in the way of our eyes and of our imaginations.

Chapter Six

MODERN HISTORY AND THE HISTORY OF THE MODERN

Alan Powers

The distinction between the two kinds of history in the title of this paper was made in an announcement of the first publication of Nikolaus Pevsner's *Outline of European Architecture*. 'The value of his achievement', said the *Architects' Journal*, 'can be summed up by saying that Dr. Pevsner has written, not the first history of modern architecture, but the first modern history of architecture.'[1] These are different things but what is their relationship?

Howard Colvin was notable among architectural historians of his generation for his practical encouragement of Modern architecture, particularly at St John's College. His work as a historian, by contrast, appears unaffected by the upheaval that Modernism represented, not only in the design of buildings, but in the education of architects and the way in which history was viewed in relationship to contemporary practice. The most one could say is that his rigorous dependence on documentation represented a sort of equivalent to a positivist attitude to structure and materials in architecture. In contrast to the earlier custom of writing about architecture in the manner of moralized *belles lettres* and aesthetic appreciation, his was an anti-rhetorical form of architectural history, building no imagined narrative structures and driving towards no teleological outcomes.

It is the period of Colvin's activity rather than himself as a historian that provides the subject for this investigation. Among his contemporaries such as John Summerson, J. M. Richards, Nikolaus Pevsner, and Reyner Banham, historical writing and the advocacy of Modernism were frequently combined. To varying degrees, these writers opened up channels of communication between the past and present, recruiting the former to give narrative continuity and hence legitimacy to selected aspects of the latter. At the same time, all these writers were engaged in a mission of public education, through popular book publishing, broadcasting, reviewing, and occasional writing, to increase the extent and depth of the audience for architecture.

Modern history, in the title of this piece, is all history written in the time of Modernism, and more particularly history written in the light of Modernism's attitude to the past. The history of Modern architecture is a specific and often problematic area within modern architectural history. Before the wider spread of

1 'Dr Nikolaus Pevsner', *Architects' Journal*, 8 April, 1943, p. 230

art history degrees in British universities, it was fair to assume that most academic architectural history would be found in schools of architecture, not an area in which Colvin was ever involved, although it could have taken his work in new directions. This suggests that potentially at least, why two strands of pedagogy in the subject should have arisen, frequently interacting but also capable of going in separate directions. Architectural history has suffered from being marginal in both types of course, and anxiety over this has led to a chain of discussions. The present essay is a brief overview of some of issues that have arisen from these discussions.

Formal architectural teaching in Britain was a late growth. The first full-time university course opened in Liverpool in 1894. In London, part-time evening courses were a longer tradition, but gradually gave way to daytime courses at the Architectural Association (AA) (1902) and UCL (1914). In 1904, when few full-time courses as yet existed, the RIBA Board of Architectural Education was convened to set standards and validate the courses for exemption from its Associateship exam. By 1914, most of the institutional structures now existing had emerged. For students, history was partly a form of practical knowledge, since they were expected to design using historical styles. For this purpose, images were more valuable than text, although their selection could indicate strong preferences and exclusions. It was exemplary, in that various lessons for design and practice could be derived indirectly from it. It was also considered part of the architect's professional equipment as a man (or woman) of learning, showing familiarity with the great buildings and names of the past.[2]

In the wake of the 'Profession or Art' controversy of 1891-92, one perceived virtue of history was that it could be taught as an examination subject and assessed more objectively than design, which was deemed unsuitable for examination by those opposed to architects' registration.[3] Architects involved in teaching in the 1890s, such as W. R. Lethaby and Beresford Pite wanted history to be filtered through the teaching of construction, rather than seen as a stand-alone subject based on books, but failed to make this a compulsory part of the RIBA guidance for schools. *A History of Architecture on the Comparative Method*, initially by the father and son combination of Professor Banister Fletcher and Banister F. Fletcher (1896 and subsequent revisions) was created primarily to meet the needs of students and proved very successful, in terms of the number of revised editions produced – averaging one every two years up to 1905. While remaining a standard

2 For an account of lecturers in architectural history in schools before 1920, see J. Mordaunt Crook, 'Architecture and History', *Architectural History* 27 (1984), pp. 555–78.

3 See T. G. Jackson and R. Norman Shaw, eds., *Architecture, a profession or an art* (London, 1892). For the history of architectural education in this period more generally, see Alan Powers, 'Architectural Education in Britain, 1880–1914' (PhD, Cambridge, 1983), and Mark Crinson and Jules Lubbock, *Architecture – art or profession?* (Manchester and New York, 1994).

work throughout the century, the rather unimaginative approach suggested the kind of rote learning and reduction of complexity that many architects wished to avoid. Bruce Allsopp wrote of Fletcher's book in 1970, 'There is no challenge to the mind, no weighing of the evidence and, by a peculiarly deadly process of illustration, all buildings, of all ages and sizes, were made to look more or less alike.'[4] Other textbooks varied the mixture. Under the influence of the Ecole des Beaux Arts, the line between history and theory became permeable, and alongside chronology there emerged a selection of paradigmatic designs leading to an understanding of typology, historical only in the sense that they came from the past, rather than being understood in a specific historical context. In England, the most sophisticated book on these lines was *Theory and Elements of Architecture* by Robert Atkinson and Hope Bagenal, 1926, which brought an Arts and Crafts understanding of materials and their performance to bear on interpreting the ancient and modern worlds, while including the role of ancient belief systems in shaping form.[5]

The apparent placidity of the 1920s was disrupted by Modernism, as progressive staff and students tried to work changes in the face of conservative resistance. History was too established in the structure to be eliminated, but Modernism raised new questions about how it should be approached. In the USA, the issue of history teaching in architecture schools was discussed in 1942 at an early meeting of what was then called the American Society of Architectural Historians. Speakers saw the need for history to adapt to meet the needs of changing architectural directions, with Henry-Russell Hitchcock stressing the importance of teaching about Modernism, but also fostering a critical approach to the whole of the past. In this sense, Modern History and the History of Modern were separate tracks that moved in parallel, driven by a new sense of purpose. In a period 'in which the greater part of architectural production is destined to be bureaucratic and anonymous', Hitchcock felt, 'many students reject *a priori* the lessons that remain to be learned from the great individual architects who have already made their mark in the twentieth century and who are, some of them, teachers in our schools.' He named Wright and Le Corbusier as examples.[6]

The scepticism of this generation of students towards history was emphasized by Robert Furneaux Jordan, who taught at the Architectural Association before and after the war. In 1946 he wrote, 'The case for not teaching architectural history to architectural students is, in the middle of the twentieth century, a very

4 Bruce Allsopp, *The Study of Architectural History* (London, 1970), p. 67.

5 See Alan Powers, 'The Classical Theory of Hope Bagenal' in Frank Salmon, ed., *The Persistence of the Classical: essays on architecture presented to David Watkin* (London, 2008), pp. 40–55.

6 Henry-Russell Hitchcock, 'Some Problems in the Interpretation of Modern Architecture', *Journal of the American Society of Architectural Historians* 2 (1942), p. 3.

strong one.'[7] Compared to the recent past in which the classical orders might move straight from the lecture screen to the drawing board, much of the history was obsolete in terms of the literal needs of the present. All that remained for Jordan was a social approach to the history of 'those times when architecture was great art', apparently to understand the conditions in which it arose rather than to analyse the art itself. A social grounding for architectural history was also emphasized by the speakers at the 1942 SAH meeting, who may have assumed that it would deter students from thinking that the past was automatically available to them. In relation to the period 1800–1950, Jordan believed that 'a diagnosis of the disease must be made', finding the causes of failure, a course also recommended by Hitchcock who wrote that rather than digging up the recent past, as historians were beginning to do, it was more important for students to find a way to bury it, although this might require the celebration of 'some fairly elaborate critical and historical rites.'[8]

Jordan advocated 'appreciation through analysis' combined with a diagnostic or sociological approach' as the only possible method.[9] He seemed unaware that while this might work in an art history course, the time available in an architecture course made it a challenging ambition. Critical of the Beaux-Arts phase for failing 'to bridge the gap between lecture theatre and studio', would his method work any better?[10]

Jordan noted that, while in 1936 at the AA, 'resistance' to the study of history was a sore point, it was negligible ten years later. Jordan asserted that the hard-won ground of Modernism might be lost if students were exposed to images of buildings that could be copied or adapted for their own work. In 1949 the architect John Brandon-Jones, who was teaching at the AA under Jordan, gave a lecture there that 'upset some of my fellow staff to such an extent that it became one of the contributory causes to my being warned to look out for another job as the AA, under new management, "is a school of 'Modern' architecture".'[11] Peter Smithson recalled that in 1941, after two years studying at Durham, the recent work by Connell, Ward and Lucas, illustrated in the *Architectural Review* and Yorke's *The Modern House in England*, was the decisive factor in changing his view of the prospects for the future of architecture, with the result that history as

[7] R. Jordan, 'The Teaching of Architectural History', *Plan*, 1949, p. 4.

[8] Hitchcock, 'Some Problems'.

[9] Jordan, 'The Teaching of Architectural History', p. 8

[10] The late Roderick Gradidge, a student in Jordan's history class at the AA c.1950, recalled an exercise in setting out a Gothic arch full size on the floor with string as part of Jordan's attempt to bring the subject to life. The exercise was hampered by the impossibility of driving a nail into the concrete floor to attach the string.

[11] John Brandon-Jones to Noel Musgrave, 23 July 1949 (Brandon-Jones papers, RIBA Archive).

taught then seemed irrelevant, 'For the first two years, it looked as if architecture was going to be a pretty boring sort of career. Then I suddenly discovered Modern Architecture and stopped going to history lectures and listening to criticisms with a clear conscience.'[12]

Modernist opposition to teaching history was seldom absolute, but it was broadly understood that new methods and material were needed. At the Bauhaus, Walter Gropius did not abolish art history, as some have been led to believe, although he wanted to restrict it to older students who, he believed, should by then have built up immunity to the possible infection of copying.[13] At Harvard, where Gropius was appointed in 1937, the Dean, Joseph Hudnut, had already begun the transformation of the course before his arrival, including a shift to studying history on the basis of construction and social issues rather than the definition and copying of styles. It was Hudnut not Gropius who removed history books as 'deadwood' from the library in Robinson Hall, where plaster casts were also removed or boxed in out of sight.[14] Even so, Gropius believed that historical study was in competition with a direct approach to understanding building technology. His emphasis on social causation was similar to the argument made by Furneaux Jordan.

If some thought history was dangerous, others simply thought it was too dull in its accustomed form. In 1941, John Summerson, who lectured regularly at the AA before and after the war, described the effect of the standard diachronic history course such as might be based on Banister Fletcher, 'always at the back of the architect's mind are those fatal categories of the examination room – Egyptian, Greek, Roman, Byzantine, Romanesque, Gothic, Renaissance – categories of death.'[15] The remark was in the context of trying to see architecture, past and present, independently of stylistic categories such as had dominated writing and teaching until then. By 1959, when Summerson contributed to a symposium on 'The value of architectural history to students of architecture' published in the *Architects' Journal*, he recognized that architectural history had been transformed since the war in 'a phase of intensity and productivity never before equaled',

[12] Peter Smithson, 'Connell, Ward and Lucas', *AA Journal*, December 1956, p. 138.

[13] See Winfried Nerdinger, 'From Bauhaus to Harvard: Walter Gropius and the use of history', in Gwendolyn Wright and Janet Parks, eds., *The History of History in American Schools of Architecture 1865–1975* (Princeton, 1990).

[14] See Jill Pearlman, 'Joseph Hudnut's Other Modernism at the "Harvard Bauhaus"', *Journal of the Society of Architectural Historians* 56 (1977), pp. 452–77, correcting aspects of Nerdinger's account, and her *Inventing American Modernism: Joseph Hudnut, Walter Gropius, and the Bauhaus legacy at Harvard* (Charlottesville, 2007).

[15] John Summerson, 'The Mischievous Analogy' (written as a lecture in 1941), in idem., *Heavenly Mansions* (London, 1949), pp. 195–218, p. 201.

making it a subject largely independent of the architectural profession.[16] What use now, he asked, was 'the old plod, plod from Brunelleschi to Bernini, from Wren to Soane'? For student purposes, he felt that history might only begin in the mid-eighteenth century with rationalist theory providing the background to the Modern Movement, the same periodization proposed by Hitchcock in 1942 that formed the basis for his volume in the Pelican History of Art. Even so, Summerson recognized that this was too limiting and that 'experience' counted even if it had no instrumental outcome. 'The student who has had his attention fixed (if only for an hour) on the contortions of Giulio Romano or the ultimate sophistications of François Mansart is better equipped than the student who has not. He is aware of the world, alive to the magic of form, in a way that the other is not.'[17] History could therefore return invigorated from its temporary absence and resume something like its old diachronic form, while animated by an altered sense of purpose. Thus, he maintained, 'the general course (the old plod, plod) is highly desirable as a means of giving a framework of experience; though its value will inevitably vary with the capacity both of the student and the teacher.'[18]

In the second contribution to the 1959 symposium, the architect and Team 10 member John Voelcker wanted architectural history taught to architects as the history of space, citing some recent examples of writing on these lines – not Pevsner's *Outline of European Architecture*, as one might have expected, but 'Smithson on Greek space, Banham on Antonio Saint'Elia, Colin Rowe and John White on perspective; or a generation earlier, Wittkower on the Centralised Church.'[19] His contribution was followed by one from Pevsner himself, who also highlighted Rudolf Wittkower's *Architectural Principles in the Age of Humanism*. Published in 1949, it become the single most important book in changing the relationship between history and modernism. Reviewing it in 1950, Voelcker wrote, 'Here history becomes an active force, part of our immediate environment, shaping our lives and forming our architecture.'[20] Reyner Banham wrote in 1955, it was 'by far the greatest contribution – for evil as well as good – by any historian to English Architecture since Pioneers of the Modern Movement.'[21] As Pevsner

16 John Summerson, 'The Value of History to Students of Architecture', *Architects' Journal,* 23 April, 1959, p. 537.

17 Ibid.

18 Ibid. It is not clear that Summerson backed this belief. According to Robin Middleton, he once stopped in the middle of a lecture on Florentine history at the AA to remark 'This is very boring, I think I will leave', which he did. (Robin Middleton, 'Obituary: Sir John Summerson', *Burlington Magazine* 135 [April 1993], pp. 277–9, p. 279).

19 John Voelcker, *Architects' Journal*, 23 April 1959, p. 538.

20 John Voelcker in *Plan* 8, 1950.

21 Reyner Banham, 'The New Brutalism', *Architectural Review*, December 1955, pp. 354–61.

described it, the effect was a fluke. There was no call from architecture schools for an analysis of Renaissance central planning or harmonic proportions, but once it was published, it offered practitioners and teachers something to fill a vacuum in theory created by the anti-formalist and instrumentalized phase of post-war Modernism, typified by the Hertfordshire Schools. This perception coincided with the first stirrings of the revolt that was confusingly named New Brutalism, itself a search for ways of re-grounding Modernism in a relationship with different aspects of the past. Almost singlehandedly, without intending to, Wittkower enabled 'modern history' to change the direction of architecture. The spectre of history encouraging students to imitate the styles of the past was laid. Wittkower's revelations about proportion synchronized with the publication of Le Corbusier's *Modulor* in 1950 (France) and 1951 (England). There was a passing fashion for mathematical proportion in architecture, but the enduring result was a new awareness that designs from the past could be approached with the same investigative and analytical rigour that architects hoped to bring to their own designs.

Pevsner raised another area of concern regarding the use of historical knowledge for conservation.[22] The kind of close reading of structures now associated with conservation seems never to have been central to history curricula, but individual teachers may well have introduced it, especially in relation to field trips and measured drawing exercises. In reality, such study seems to have been self-directed by students, aided by publications by Ronald Brunskill of the Manchester University School of Architecture and other writers.[23] Despite the considerable increase in architects' work relating to old buildings, it is still not considered as part of degree or diploma courses in architecture schools.

As the author who, above all others, extended architectural history to a wide non-specialist readership, Pevsner made the case for architectural history because it was a universal need, not because it was specifically needed by students of architecture. In the thirteen years between Jordan's *Plan* article of 1946 and the *Architects' Journal* Symposium of 1959, architectural history achieved a general currency in Britain that could never have been imagined before the war. Then as now, students of architecture might well know less history than a number of people with a general interest in the arts. Rather than worrying about being in line with student needs or expectations, Pevsner believed that teachers of history should present it as an independent enriching discipline based on knowledge and objectivity, appealing in its style of delivery but not pandering to the students.

22 Pevsner also addressed the lack of appropriate training for conservation work in 'The Training of Architects, Interim Survey', *Architectural Review*, June 1950, p. 372

23 R. W. Brunskill, *Illustrated Handbook of Vernacular Architecture* (London, 1971).

The idea that the present might alter not only the view of the past but in effect the past itself, was beginning to dawn. Colin Rowe, whose first articles in this mode anticipated Wittkower and showed the parallels between classicism and modernism more explicitly, continued to develop his own work and to inspire others to let Modernism open a new set of windows on the past.[24] It could even be said that the disjunction between history and Modernism was instantly overcome. Rowe and his associates, starting with the 'Texas rangers', were in Robert Maxwell's words, 'a band of teachers who saw a way of teaching modernity consistently with traditional architectural principles.'[25]

The final contributor to the 1959 symposium was Reyner Banham, trained as a historian at the Courtauld and under Pevsner, then employed at the *Architectural Review*, but recruited in 1964 to teach history at the Bartlett School, University College London. Banham denied the possibility of grounding a theory of modern architecture on the study of the past and limited the role of the historian in architectural education to the 'close cultural background, including pedigree of ideas and movements currently effective in architecture.'[26] This was the material that he published in 1960 as *Theory and Design in the First Machine Age*. Unusually, Banham advocated history as a means of learning about professional practice, but finished his remarks by two demands: to stop the teaching of history by unqualified historians (thus excluding the design teachers who undertook the task in most schools), and the end of 'the teaching of history as an academic discipline to students who are not going to practise that discipline.' The latter is puzzling: if not an academic discipline (as it would presumably be for a qualified historian), then what else might it be? Perhaps the paradox was a deliberate challenge from someone not yet engaged in the situation. Banham curiously continued to doubt his own value as a historian, as if that were necessary to retain his credibility among the creative group with whom he associated, who probably did not share this view. Claiming that technology was the defining characteristic of Modernism's future, he stood at the opposite end of a spectrum from Colin Rowe and the other critical historians, such as Alan Colquhoun, Joseph Rykwert, and Kenneth Frampton, all trained as architects, who were developing the answer to the question of what new form history might take in the wake of Modernism without becoming irrelevant. Their particular approach was given much greater scope in the leading schools in America, while Rykwert's influential teaching at

[24] Rowe's most influential articles remained his first two in the *Architectural Review*: 'The Mathematics of the Ideal Villa', March 1947, and 'Mannerism and Modern Architecture', May 1950.

[25] Robert Maxwell, 'Rowe, Colin Frederick (1920–1999)' in *Oxford Dictionary of National Biography*.

[26] Reyner Banham in *Architects' Journal* 23 April 1959, p. 540.

the University of Essex was in an art history school rather than an architecture course.

Banham was a contributor to another discussion of the same subject at the 1964 American Institute of Architects and Association of Collegiate Schools of Architecture teacher seminar, held at Cranbrook College, Detroit and published in book form by MIT the following year. At this point, Banham's contention that technology was the main issue was considered paramount in the book's introduction by Buford L. Pickens, who wrote, 'the committee felt a pressing need to reconsider in a new light the sources of humanizing potentials for architecture in our era when the pervasive influence of science with all its automated technology tends to make lessons from the past seem irrelevant.'[27] The same text dismisses the old fear about infection from history as obsolete, recognizing, perhaps in the light of Rowe's writings, that the masters of modernism achieved their success through knowledge of history rather than through ignorance of it.

The contributions to the book bring forward concerns about theory that were not present in 1959 in the *Architects' Journal*. That theory was an issue in 1964 may be due to two causes. First, the onward path of architecture was turning out not to be as straight as expected. Around 1960, various trends were noted, such as a new classicizing tendency, especially in America, 'Neo-Liberty' in Italy, criticized by Banham, and what Pevsner, in his well-known lecture called 'The Return of Historicism' in 1961.[28] Pevsner's contention was that the reflection of certain forms, mainly from around 1900, were re-emerging in recent designs for buildings and furniture. In taking such strong exception to these, and upholding as an ideal a pure version of inter-war Modernism, Pevsner recognized the beginnings of post-modernism (a phrase he used in his text).

According to John Summerson's assessment in his 1957 lecture, 'The Case for a Modern Theory of Architecture', if there was a theory of architecture, it failed to supply a formal language. Realising this was part of Modernism's ageing pains, Peter Smithson said in response to Summerson's paper: 'I think that the old-type modern architecture is stuck between practice and discontent; it is round about the academicisation point.'[29] A similar argument was made by Christopher Alexander in the *Architect's Year Book* in an article entitled 'The Revolution finished twenty years ago' that reflected his own frustration as a student at

[27] Buford L. Pickens, 'Foreword' in Marcus Whiffen, ed., *The History, Theory and Criticism of Architecture* (Cambridge MA, 1965), p. vii.

[28] Reyner Banham, 'History under Revision', *Architectural Review* 127, May 1960, pp. 325–332; Nikolaus Pevsner, 'Modern Architecture and the Historian or the Return of Historicism', *RIBA Journal* 68, April 1961, pp. 230–40.

[29] Peter Smithson, contribution to discussion on 21 May 1957, *RIBA Journal* 64, June 1957, p. 312.

Cambridge with the assumption that the same creative impulses that drove people in the 1920s could still be harnessed in such a changed world.[30]

One of the contributors to the 1964 symposium, Bruno Zevi, confronted the presumption that had prevailed during the previous 30 years or more that history and practice should be separated. 'Given the fact that you cannot have a coherent school of architecture unless you reach a real integration between history and design, we have reached the nadir.'[31] The old language of architecture had not been replaced by a new one and the only method for criticizing student schemes was a weak, vague version of personal taste. A renewed form of history could serve a different and more significant role in stiffening things up. 'Design is going to be taught in the history courses ... and history is going to be taught at the drafting tables. This is the challenge for all of us. We have to merge history and design courses, renewing the methods of both.'[32] In Zevi's view, modern history was not to become exclusively the history of Modern, but it would be recalibrated to suit the needs of an emerging post-modernism. As Stanford Anderson later commented, 'Zevi's advocacy of an operative architectural history and the virtual takeover of schools by historians did not precisely carry the day.'[33]

At Cranbrook in 1964, Banham emphasized the different and diverging views among the academic community at the time about history and theory. He suggested that architectural theory might constitute the kind of extrapolation from the designs of the past that could be applied harmlessly enough to the student design experience, since the specifics of historic style would have been purged from it, as happened with Wittkower's work in the 1950s. His view that everything in architecture should bow to progress in technology was contested by Stanford Anderson, in a paper given at the Architectural Association in 1963, in which he imagined alternative positions between the irreconcilable opposites of Modernism and tradition depicted by Banham. He cited Karl Popper in support of a more critical view of a theory such as the necessary dominance of technology, and suggested that tradition could be both strengthened and detoxified if approached in a suitably critical spirit.

In what Spiro Kostof called 'a history-affirming period' after the publication of Robert Venturi's *Complexity and Contradiction* and the passage of the Historic Preservation Act in 1966, new relationships between architecture, education, and

30 Christopher Alexander, 'The Revolution finished twenty years ago', in Trevor Dannatt, ed., *Architect's Year Book 9* (London, 1957).

31 Bruno Zevi, 'History as a method of teaching architecture', in Whiffen, ed., *The History, Theory, and Criticism of Architecture*, p.14

32 Ibid., p. 19.

33 Stanford Anderson, 'Architectural History in Schools of Architecture', *Journal of the Society of Architectural Historians* 58 (1999), pp. 282–90, p. 284.

history were emerging in the USA, and were mirrored in Britain.[34] This was principally owing to a new type of exponent, the 'architect-historian', a historian closer to the process of design than the art historian, but given a new distance from it by the growth of analytic method, for which Rowe provided one of the models, but for which others were then emerging. As Stanford Anderson wrote in 1999, their training as architects 'provided a degree of technical competence that was advantageous to the study of architecture, but perhaps more importantly it provided a mentality more open to speculation.'[35] In some cases, the actual printed presentation of their work developed from earlier models, showing how the placing of illustrations and the design of a spread of text and images was part of the non-verbal means of communication. This new group, whose work was found in journals such as *Oppositions* and *Assemblage*, covered various areas of subject and method. There was an emphasis on digging deeper into the origins of Modernism and altering the received narrative while emphasizing the significance of a wider range of historical figures. Thus the history of the Modern has, predictably, extended from the small canon of literature and evidence available in the 1970s to become an exponentially spreading coverage within which much still remains to be achieved.

All this happened in Howard Colvin's working life, but owing to the clear direction he had set himself and the nature of his teaching, institutionally allied to history rather than art history, and far distant from any architectural students, it can hardly be said to have impinged either on his writing or his teaching. Even if there is no intention to teach history instrumentally, the division in teaching style between academic historians in architecture and art history schools inevitably and properly remains, and arguably adds richness and three-dimensionality to the discipline as a whole.

34 Spiro Kostof, 'The Shape of Time at Yale, c.1960', in Wright and Parks, eds., *The History of History in American Schools of Architecture*, p. 123.

35 Anderson, 'Architectural History in Schools of Architecture', p. 284.

Chapter Seven

COLVIN AND THE CONSERVATION MOVEMENT

Malcolm Airs

Like many of his contemporaries, conservation and Howard Colvin were not automatic bed fellows. Nevertheless, without his meticulous scholarship, the influential conservation movement which flourished from the 1960s onwards would have lacked much of the intellectual credibility which was one of its most powerful weapons. His pivotal role in establishing the firm academic foundations of architectural history was crucial in creating a more refined sensibility and understanding of the inherited built environment.

Yet, unlike the two other members of the knighted trinity of architectural historians of his generation – Pevsner and Summerson – he took no public part in the great conservation battles of the day. Both of those titans could, of course, be equivocal allies. Summerson's record on St Pancras, the Palumbo proposals for No 1 Poultry, and the demolition of parts of Bloomsbury, amply demonstrate that he was not a natural recruit to the cause. And, for all those countless buildings that were saved at Public Inquiry as a result of a choice phrase in the *Buildings of England*, there were several others that were condemned by a disparaging comment from Pevsner's pen.

As far as I am aware, Colvin never appeared as an expert witness at a Public Inquiry either in support or in opposition to a development proposal. His unassuming demeanour, perhaps, was not suited to such a role. Nor did he lend his signature easily to a letter of protest. His contribution was much more subtle and largely played out behind the scenes. Nevertheless it was often hugely influential. It was in the world of committees that he excelled – both at a national and at a local level. And it was the future of the country house that deeply exercised him.

He was a member of the Royal Fine Art Commission from 1962 to 1972. Although this was not primarily a conservation body, during that period it increasingly began to take a stance on heritage issues as well as matters of architectural design. In 1973 he was appointed a Commissioner on the Royal Commission on the Historical Monuments of England, in which role he remained for the next thirteen years. Within two years, beginning with Eric Mercer's *English Vernacular Houses*, the Commission began to take the first tentative steps towards publishing synthetic volumes that engaged with a broader understanding of architectural history alongside the dry lists in the county inventories. The timing of the arrival of Colvin at these two institutions and these fresh initiatives might just have been a coincidence and we can only surmise as to whether he helped to shape them or not. But his influence on the Historic Buildings Council of England (HBC) is not open to doubt. He joined the Council in 1970 and he continued to serve it until it was wound up in 1984. He was then appointed to its successor body, English Heritage.

One of Howard's last publications was a brief history of the role played by the Council in addressing the threats posed to the survival of the country house in the second half of the twentieth century which formed the focus of much of its work. The sheer pleasure that he had enjoyed in those early post-war years in the company of Rupert Gunnis, Lawrence Stone, and John Harris when they were seeking out abandoned or neglected country houses is vividly captured in his opening paragraph when he reflected on

> Those, who like myself, drove or bicycled down potholed drives, never knowing what one would find at the end: sometimes a ruin, sometimes a surprised owner still in residence, sometimes a deserted house whose windows were not merely unfastened ... but whose front door could be pushed open to reveal a chaos of abandoned papers ... a large collection of Roman alters ... or even more disconcertingly, a flock of chickens or a herd of pigs in occupation of the state rooms. The idea that their ancestral homes were an important part of the national heritage was still far from the minds of many owners.[1]

He recounts with amusement that Gunnis was given a set of porphyry busts of Roman emperors which were languishing in a chicken run at Goodwood and how he found Lord Ferrers attempting to 'shoot the balls' off the lead statues at Staunton Harold. Howard's own garden in Plantation Road was adorned with several trophies from these forays.

As the only source of state funding to private owners at the time, the HBC and its offshoot the Historic Buildings Bureau, were of crucial importance in encouraging owners in the repair of their buildings. It recognised that 'occupancy was the key to maintenance, and if the original owner had gone it was imperative to find a new – and that generally meant an institutional – owner.'[2] The fact that so many country houses have survived into an age when they are more highly valued – and an increasing number have reverted from institutional use back to private ownership – is due in no small measure to the encouragement of the HBC at this critical point in their history.

The Council was only empowered to give grants to buildings that were considered outstanding and Colvin applauded 'the exacting critical standards' of

[1] H. M. Colvin, 'The Historic Buildings Council and the Country House', in Malcolm Airs, ed., *The Great House in the Twentieth Century* (Oxford, 2002), pp. 101–8, p. 101.

[2] Ibid., p. 105.

7.1. Calke Abbey, Derbyshire (Malcolm Airs, 1995).

Summerson as 'a salutary check to over-enthusiastic assessments of candidates for grant' adding 'he enjoyed playing the part of Devil's advocate when some marginally "outstanding" building came up for consideration'.[3]

The Council stoutly resisted any attempt to set down in writing the criteria for outstanding status. In Colvin's view 'this was a matter for collective judgement'. That judgement in Colvin's time on the Council amongst others was exercised by such distinguished historians as Pevsner, John Cornforth, Dorothy Stroud, Mark Girouard, and David Watkin, as well as by Summerson and himself.

In addition to making grants for repair and maintenance, the HBC had the responsibility of advising government on the acquisition of houses of major importance, usually in lieu of Death Duties, which were then passed on to the National Trust. When Colvin was on the Council, Cragside and Calke Abbey were acquired in this way. But they singularly failed to convince the Minister of the value of Mentmore in 1976 – a house which Colvin himself considered to be of 'marginal quality' but redeemed by what he described as its 'fabulous contents'.[4]

His most personal intervention was in the rescue of Calke (fig. 7.1), although in his published account of the house he modestly plays down his role. He first

[3] Ibid., p. 104.
[4] Ibid., p. 107.

visited the house in the company of Rupert Gunnis in 1964, as amusingly described by John Harris; but it was in March 1981 with the death of Charles Harpur-Crewe that the full extent of the crisis affecting the estate emerged. Harpur-Crewe had died without making a will, and a life-interest in the estate passed to his unmarried brother Henry together with a tax liability of nearly £10m. The battle to save the house with its extraordinary contents immediately commenced although it was to take a further three years of vigorous campaigning before it was to reach a successful conclusion.

Although less than 5 years had elapsed since the refusal to acquire Mentmore, by 1981 informed public opinion had significantly shifted. As Colvin wrote in relation to Calke:

> Conservation had become a national preoccupation, almost a political force. Within the 'Establishment', the National Heritage Memorial Fund, the Historic Buildings Council, the Parliamentary Heritage Group, and the National Trust itself, all urged the government to think again, while outside it every newspaper and every television company featured the plight of the 'time-capsule house'.[5]

When finally in March 1984, Nigel Lawson, as Chancellor of the Exchequer, announced the provision of the necessary funds to save Calke Abbey it was, as Howard pointed out, 'the first time that the claims of conservation and the heritage had been formally recognised in a Budget speech'.[6] Whilst acknowledging the efforts of others, including SAVE and the Harpur-Crewe trustees, the determined advocacy of Colvin contributed enormously to this achievement.

In 1984 the responsibilities of the HBC were transferred to the newly-formed English Heritage where Howard was appointed a Commissioner and chaired its advisory committee. In a retrospective comment written in 2002 he noted with evident satisfaction that 'whatever else the HBC achieved in the 29 years of its existence, it had certainly fulfilled its original remit of saving as many country houses as possible.' He could not resist, however, taking a characteristic swipe at some of the more purist conservation principles which had been adopted by a later generation when he observed that 'where the demolition of later accretions reduced a house to a more manageable size, or removed additions of doubtful architectural merit, the HBC was generally tolerant of amputation'. Adding that

> the doctrine that every addition must be preserved because it is part of the history of the house had not yet become conservationist gospel, and to a body acutely aware of the problems facing country house owners it might seem to be just as much part of the history of a house to demolish an unwanted addition in the 20th century as it had been to add it in the 19th.[7]

5 Howard Colvin, *Calke Abbey, Derbyshire. A hidden house revealed* (London, 1985), p. 82.
6 Ibid., p. 83.
7 Colvin, 'The Historic Buildings Council', p. 108.

An illuminating case of which he greatly approved was Heydon Hall in Norfolk (fig. 7.2). Largely built in the early-seventeenth century, it was enlarged to either side in the late-eighteenth century and again in the nineteenth in a rather rambling manner which Pevsner pithily dismissed as 'a pity'.[8] It came to the HBC in 1973 with a proposal to reduce the house to its original form. This was enthusiastically supported by the Council which offered a substantial grant for the repair of the house. Such drastic surgery to a neglected house would have aroused far more soul-searching today, but there can be little doubt that in the case of Heydon it re-introduced an architectural coherence and succeeded magnificently in rejuvenating the whole estate and its associated village and parkland at a time when its future was uncertain.[9]

In castigating an automatic application of the doctrine of 'conserve as found', I have no doubt that Howard was indeed thinking of Heydon. He certainly used it as a precedent in considering the problem of Barrington Park in Gloucestershire when it came to the advisory committee of English Heritage in the very changed circumstances of 1999 (fig. 7.3). The core of the house was built by William Smith of Warwick in 1737–38. The two flanking symmetrical wings were added in 1873 by J. Macvicar Anderson. Here money for the repair of the house and the maintenance of the estate was not the principal issue. Rather it was the dislike of the defiant owner for the nineteenth-century wings and his hatred of the bureaucratic mechanisms which were imposed on the owners of listed buildings. In response to a repairs notice served by the local authority, he grudgingly scaffolded the eighteenth-century part of the house but adamantly refused to provide any protection over the roofs of the later wings despite being denied permission to demolish them at a Public Inquiry. Initially the views of the panel were divided but Howard skilfully brokered a compromise by persuading the son of the owner to engage Peter Inskip as his professional adviser. As a result, a proper conservation plan was drawn up for the whole estate which proposed the repair of the important eighteenth-century garden buildings and the refurbishment of the estate cottages in the village. In return a much more sympathetic proposal for the reduction of the house was eventually approved. Although this might not have pleased the supporters of Macvicar Anderson and it certainly would not comply with the current *Conservation Principles* adopted by English Heritage in 2008, it bought time for a proper consideration of the estate as a whole and the commencement of a wider programme of repair. Ironically, twelve years on, a fresh application which retains the wings has recently been submitted by the son who has duly inherited the estate.

8 Nikolaus Pevsner, *the Buildings of England: North-East Norfolk and Norwich* (Harmondsworth, 1962), p. 164.

9 For the full story see John Cornforth, *The Country Houses of England 1948–1998* (London, 1998), pp. 37–40, 313–16.

7.2. Heydon Hall, Norfolk, after the removal of the flanking wings (Malcolm Airs, 1996)

7.3. The advisory committee of English Heritage on a site visit to Barrington Park, Gloucestershire in 1999 (Malcolm Airs).

It was not just in the debates on such issues between the distinguished members of the advisory committee that Colvin's influence was felt. Many of the officers who served the committee – and the HBC before it – had been trained by him: either directly at Oxford or indirectly through the strict academic standards of the *Dictionary*. The presentations of individual cases to the committee were conducted almost like tutorials and the intellectual calibre of the discussion was very high with Howard adopting the role of Devil's advocate that had previously been played by Summerson within the HBC. Howard was always very supportive of younger scholars and generous in promoting their careers. In my own case, it was only after my undergraduate years that he succeeded in adding an architectural history special subject to the Oxford syllabus, but I did attend his post-graduate classes on the sources for architectural history. And he taught me the techniques of building analysis on his field trips into the parish churches of the Oxfordshire countryside armed only with a blank plan that we were required to annotate prior to a rigorous discussion of the evidence for our conclusions. Later I worked closely with him in the 1970s when I was secretary of the Listed Buildings Committee of the Oxford Architectural and Historical Society (OAHS) which commented on planning applications in the county. Although he never said so, I am positive that he was instrumental in my appointment to the English Heritage advisory committee in 1988, not as an additional architectural historian but to give a voice to the local authority conservation movement.

In addition to case-work, grant-giving, and strategic policy, one of the other responsibilities of the committee was to offer advice to the government on the then contentious subject of the listing of post-war buildings. I remember a particularly robust discussion about the Queen Elizabeth Hall on the South Bank. Howard was no great admirer of its concrete Brutalism but with typical intellectual detachment he recognised its significance as part of a brief architectural movement of some importance and probably the last public concert hall to be financed and built by a local authority. Despite his aesthetic distaste, he pressed strongly for its listing – although the recommendation failed to find favour with successive Secretaries of State.

His influence on the conservation movement was not just confined to the national stage. At a local level, he was briefly a trustee of the Oxford Preservation Trust and for many years he chaired the listed buildings committee of the OAHS with tact and diplomacy. His experience with the HBC and English Heritage was invaluable in ensuring that the representations from the Society were measured and focused and the committee effectively provided a conservation service to the county at a time before 1974 when the planning authority had no professional expertise in the discipline.

In 1990, he was a member of the validation panel which established the

7.4. Haunt Hill House, Great Weldon, Northamptonshire (Malcolm Airs, 2011).

Masters degree in Historic Conservation at the then Oxford Polytechnic. His major contribution to its proceedings was to insist that the syllabus was firmly based on the study of architectural history. I was the direct beneficiary of that insistence because when the degree came into being in the following year it was a pioneering joint venture between Oxford University and Oxford Brookes and, with Howard as one of my referees, I was appointed to teach the history modules and to develop the programme at Rewley House which finally introduced a post-graduate qualification in architectural history to the University of Oxford.

Colvin's architectural enthusiasms were, of course, highly selective. Above all else, it was the country house and those buildings which demonstrated the soundly-attributed hand of the professional architect that excited him. The polite rather than the vernacular or utilitarian, although he was always willing to listen to the views of others with more catholic tastes. It was probably his great Oxford companions Peter Spokes and Billy Pantin who first directed him to Haunt Hill House in Northamptonshire, his only published venture into the field of vernacular architecture (fig. 7.4). They contributed the plans and the photographs of this modest house whilst he burrowed into the archives to establish the connection

Fig. 7.5. The White Hart Inn, Fyfield, Berkshire (Malcolm Airs).

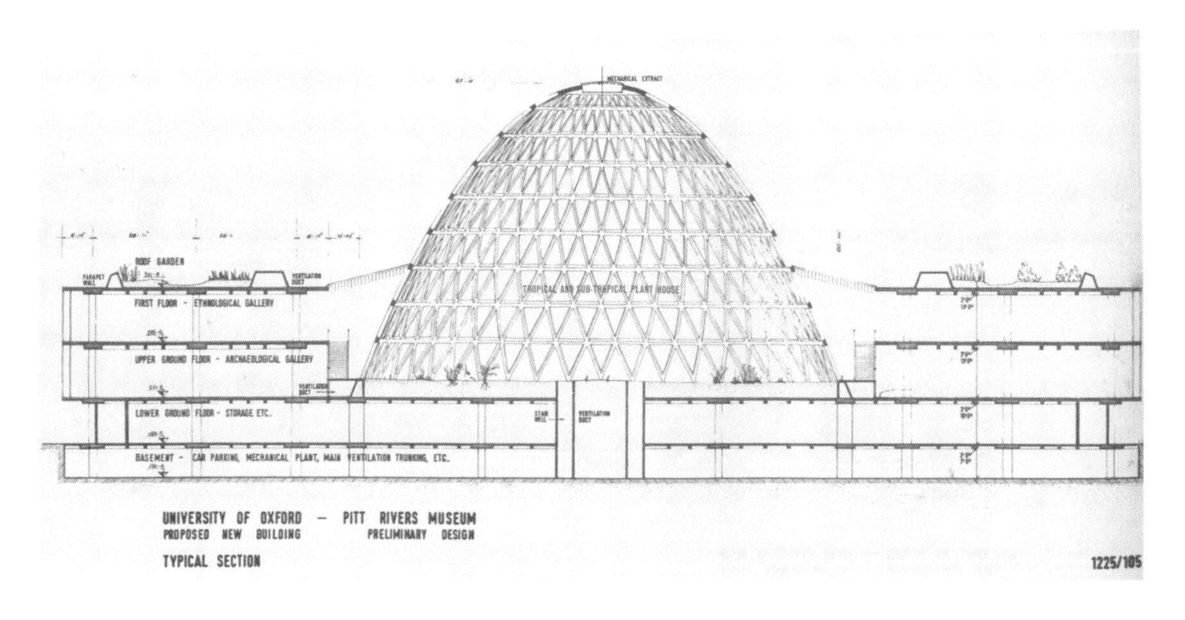

Fig. 7.6. Section through the proposed Pitt Rivers Museum, Oxford (Estates Services, University of Oxford, January 1967).

with the Frisby and Grumbold families of master masons that explained the remarkable decoration.[10]

It was a phone call from Spokes that alerted Colvin to the imminent removal of the fifteenth-century roof at the college property of the White Hart at Fyfield during the restoration of 1963 and which prompted his intervention to save it (fig. 7.5). At English Heritage, a rash of applications for grants to repair windmills led him to encourage Ron Brunskill to draw up a list of criteria by which the committee could judge the individual significance of each case and henceforward 'the Brunskill scale' was rigorously applied.

It would be totally wrong to try and label Colvin simply as a critical advocate for the conservation cause. Although he was dedicated to an understanding of the architecture of the past, he was far too interested in the visionary potential of new architecture to adopt such a limited stance. His *Unbuilt Oxford* makes that abundantly clear where he characterises Oxford dons as an 'architecturally retarded body, too much concerned to preserve and too little willing to create'. He devoted the last chapter in the book to Oxford and the Modern Movement and concluded with two abortive projects of the 1960s. With Chamberlin, Powell and Bon's 25-storey Zoology tower proposed for the University Parks he had little sympathy but he genuinely regretted the failure to raise the funds necessary to build Pier Luigi Nervi's striking Pitt-Rivers museum in the Banbury Road designed in conjunction with Powell and Moya (fig. 7.6). This he saw as 'perhaps the last chance for the university to build in the twentieth century something that would take its place with the Divinity School, the Radcliffe Library and the Ashmolean Museum as a major work of European architecture'.[11]

The scheme involved the demolition of three Victorian villas on St John's Norham Manor Estate. No. 60 Banbury Road by William Wilkinson was built in 1869, no. 62 (fig. 7.7) by E. G. Bruton with a sculpted pediment by J. Hungerford Pollen for the Revd. R. St J. Tyrwhitt – friend and secretary to Ruskin – was built in 1865 (fig. 7.8), and no. 64, also by Bruton, dated from 1873. Planning permission for the demolition of all three was duly granted but by the early 1970s, when it was clear that Nervi's design would not be realised, there had been a marked change in the appreciation of the architectural and townscape qualities of the North Oxford estate. Parts of it were designated as the first conservation area in the city in 1968 although the line was drawn to exclude the Pitt-Rivers site. In the same year 62 Banbury Road was listed. By 1972 the conservation area had been extended in a manner which effectively blocked the scheme and no. 60 was

[10] H. M. Colvin, 'Haunt Hill House, Weldon', in E. M. Jope, ed., *Studies in Building History* (London, 1961), pp. 223–28.

[11] H. M. Colvin, *Unbuilt Oxford* (New Haven and London, 1983), ch. 10.

Fig. 7.7. 62 Banbury Road, Oxford (Malcolm Airs, 2013).

Fig. 7.8. Entrance sculpture, 62 Banbury Road, Oxford (Malcolm Airs, 2013).

Fig. 7.9. Proposed Pitt Rivers Museum, sketch from the Banbury Road (Estates Services, University of Oxford, January 1967).

Fig. 7.10. St Anne's College, Oxford (Elain Harwood, 2001), and enlarged detail showing Sir Howard Colvin.

added to the list. Instead of Colvin's 'spectacular architectural concept which would have delighted many besides anthropologists' (fig. 7.9), the University built a modest single story annex at the rear of no 60 designed by Eric Powell for the University Surveyor. This, in turn, was skilfully adapted by the local architectural practice of Berman Gueddes Stretten in 2008 to provide the dining facilities for Kellogg College which now occupies the whole site. With an irony that Howard would have appreciated, Wilkinson's villa at the front is now the home of the College's Centre for the Historic Environment.

Given his enthusiasm for creative modern design, it is appropriate to conclude with an image taken by Elain Harwood of Howard standing in front of Howell, Killick, Partridge and Amis's 1966 gatehouse to St Anne's College on the Woodstock Road (fig. 7.10). His support for its listing was, I think, his last intervention on behalf of the conservation movement – and, like the Queen Elizabeth Hall, it failed to convince the Secretary of State.

Chapter Eight

MONUMENTAL HISTORY: *THE HISTORY OF THE KING'S WORKS*

Simon Thurley

The towering achievement of Sir Howard Colvin's *Biographical Dictionary* has, perhaps, overshadowed his other monumental work *The History of the King's Works*, the multi-volume and multi-authored chronicle of the English Office of Works.[1] The history was, in its own way, a pioneering work of scholarship which deserves to be better understood and this paper describes the genesis and execution of the book and assesses its significance.[2]

Twentieth-century Whitehall was no stranger to institutional history. In the 1920s a series of volumes known as the *Whitehall Series* had been produced chronicling the history of the principal Offices of State. Twelve volumes had been published by 1935 by which time more pressing matters were emerging and the series ground to a halt.[3] As a consequence the volume on Office of Works remained unwritten. In the late 1940s there was a strong awareness that many government departments, including the Office of Works, had been transformed by the Second World War and the government commissioned a second series of official histories, called the *United Kingdom Civil Series* which chronicled the departmental history of the War. It was edited by Professor Sir Keith Hancock who had been Chichele Professor of Economic History at Oxford.[4] The volume on the Office of Works was written by Major Charles Kohan, official historian to the Cabinet Secretariat, whose only book this was.[5] Hancock and Kohan agreed

1 H. M. Colvin, ed., *The History of the King's Works*, I & II, 'The Middle Ages', R. Allen Brown, H. M. Colvin, and A. J. Taylor (London, 1963); III (Part I), '1485–1660', H. M. Colvin, D. R. Ransome, and John Summerson (London, 1975); IV (Part II), '1485–1660', H. M. Colvin, John Summerson, Martin Biddle, J. R. Hale, and Marcus Merriman, (London 1982); V, '1660–1782'; H. M. Colvin, J. Mordaunt Crook, Kerry Downes, and John Newman (London, 1976); VI, '1782–1851', J. Mordaunt Crook and M. H. Port (London, 1973).

2 The English Heritage registry (reference AA 019042/1 parts 1–13 and 29 & 30; AA 019042/1/1; AM 000005/006/ part 1; AE009531/1) contains the complete set of files covering the King's Works project from its inception to the publication of the last volume in 1982. The text of this paper is based on the files which are not paginated. Additional sources are footnoted separately.

3 Health (1925), Home Office (1925), Colonial Office (1926), India Office (1926), Education (1927), Post Office (1927), Agriculture and Fisheries (1927), The Treasury (1927), Board of Trade (1928), Scotland yard (1929), Foreign Office (1933), War Office (1935).

4 K. S. Inglis, 'Hancock, Sir William Keith', *Oxford Dictionary of National Biography*.

5 *Who Was Who* on-line edition 2011.

that the volume on the Office of Works which had, of course, been reborn as the Ministry of Works in October 1940, should cover only its activities in serving the war effort rather than its entire scope of responsibilities which included, for instance, the care of ancient monuments and historic buildings. Thus Kohan's book, published in 1952 was entitled *Works and Buildings* and covered the ministry's war-related activities only.[6]

In 1949 Sir Edward Bridges,[7] Permanent Secretary at the Treasury and Head of the Civil Service, made the suggestion that with so many changes within Whitehall there should be a new series of Whitehall histories. This was music to the ears of Sir Harold Emmerson, the Permanent Secretary to the Office of Works.[8] Emmerson was a career civil servant who had joined as a second-division clerk. For ten years from 1946 he was in charge of the Ministry of Works where amongst other things he was responsible for the detailed arrangements for the coronation. Emmerson was concerned that the public understand the civil service, its functions and services, and championed a series of guides that explained this.

Two years into his job at the Ministry of Works he had approached the publishers J. M. Dent to see whether they might be interested in a short history of the Office of Works. Dent's turned him down suggesting he try *Country Life* and approach Sir John Summerson as author. Bridges's suggestion of a new Whitehall series was thus seized by Emmerson. 1951 was the centenary of the establishment of the Commissioners of Works and he wanted a book to come out in time for this. Spurred on by the thought of the new series he approached Fredric Raby, a former member of the Inspectorate of Ancient Monuments who had gone on to be a fellow at Jesus College Cambridge, and asked him to write a short history.[9] Raby, by now more interested in medieval Latin verse, turned him down. But Emmerson had got the bit between his teeth and was thinking of two books. One on the early history of the Office of Works, a work 'of scholarship based upon research', and another which would be a brochure distributed widely giving an outline of the department's history and present functions.

So the matter was remitted to a Committee headed by the Chairman of the Board of Works. It first met in February 1951 and within the space of a couple of hours it was agreed that the work would be one of major scholarship and that it would take between five and ten years to research and write and that their preferred editor was F. J. Raby. The Public Records Office were asked for their cooperation; they welcomed the project as it closely aligned with one of their own

6 C. M. Kohan, *Works and Buildings* (London, 1952).
7 Richard A. Chapman 'Bridges, Edward Ettingdene', *Oxford Dictionary of National Biography.*
8 Rodney Lowe, 'Emmerson, Sir Harold Corti', *Oxford Dictionary of National Biography.*
9 *Who was Who* on-line edition 2011.

to publish new guides to the records including a volume on the Works which was then in draft.[10]

Their immediate idea was to ask John Harvey to write the medieval sections.[11] He was the obvious choice as he had been studying the Works accounts in the PRO and the wills at Somerset House since the 1930s and had been in the Office of Works before the war. There was a problem however. Harvey had been dismissed from the Office of Works after declaring as a conscientious objector and was imprisoned in Wormwood Scrubs. Such was the memory of the Office in 1949 that Harvey was quite out of the question as the main man.

Despite a second invitation, Raby was still not to be wooed and this gave the second Committee meeting the task of identifying an alternative editor. Two men on the Committee would have been eminently qualified, Arnold Taylor, the Inspector for Wales,[12] and George Chettle, the Inspector for London, who had written the *Survey of London* volume on the Queen's House in 1937.[13] But as they were both full time employees of the Board it was felt that they would not have the time. Instead Arnold Taylor and Bryan St. John O'Neil, the Chief Inspector,[14] both recommended a certain Mr. Colvin.[15] Colvin's name was already known to the assistant keeper from the PRO, J. H. Collingridge, and to George Chettle and it was agreed in March 1951 that Arnold Taylor should ask him to be editor.

By the end of March Colvin had accepted the commission but said that he wanted to think about who his contributors would be. This was to be an ongoing preoccupation for thirty years as he struggled to extract contributions from collaborators who were, in extreme cases, five or six years late with their text. Several contributors were relieved of their duties part way through, while those who had performed well were given additional sections to write. Some initially put forward as collaborators were vetoed by Colvin for their lack of academic credentials, their poor literary style, or for being too 'art historical'. Those, whose names eventually graced the title pages, like attributions in the *Dictionary*, had

10 For the P.R.O. programme see D. Knowles, 'Great Historical Enterprises, IV: The Rolls Series', *Transactions of the Royal Historical Society*, 5 ser. (1961), pp. 137–59.

11 David Brock, 'Harvey, John Hooper', *Oxford Dictionary of National Biography*.

12 A. Saunders, 'Taylor, Arnold Joseph', *Oxford Dictionary of National Biography*.

13 *Who was Who* on-line edition 2011.

14 *Who was Who* on line edition 2011.

15 Throughout I have taken biographical details of Sir Howard's life from, William Whyte, 'Colvin, Howard Montagu', *Oxford Dictionary of National Biography*; Richard Hewlings, 'Sir Howard Colvin (1919–2007)', *Society of Architectural Historians of Great Britain Newsletter* 94 (Summer 2008), pp. 1–4; J. Mordaunt Crook, 'Howard Montagu Colvin, 1919–2007', *Proceedings of the British Academy*, 166 (2010), pp. 119–132; John Newman, 'Sir Howard Colvin', *The Guardian*, 15 January 2008.

passed Colvin's most stringent tests. Two people were key to the whole project, Sir John Summerson[16] and Arnold Taylor, who both contributed sections – in the case of Summerson many sections – but who were also crucial to sustaining the dogged determination behind the whole enterprise.

The contributors never met for editorial meetings, there was no board or committee, just a direct one-to-one relationship with the editor. He, in turn, was the sole contact with the Ministry of Works, or as it became the Department of Ancient Monuments and Historic Buildings of the Department of the Environment. So Colvin, in August 1951, Joined the Ministry's Steering Committee and planning began. At this point it is worth noting that the other elements of Emmerson's original plan did come to fruition; a brochure was indeed published for more general use[17] and Emmerson himself wrote a volume for the New Whitehall Series on the Ministry of Works. Reviewed by the *Daily Telegraph*, it was dubbed 'a dry, competent book', a plaudit that he perhaps did not cherish.[18]

Over the following meetings the steering group decided that the work would cover from the twelfth century to 1852 with a brief epilogue and was to be three volumes of 300,000 words apiece. The purpose of the book was to trace the history of building as an exercise of royal authority and it was clear that the individual histories of each building were a route to this and never primarily a stylistic or functional analysis of the site in question. This was at heart institutional history. From the beginning it was assumed that the history of the Office of Works ended in 1851 when its duties were taken over by a Government Department subject to full Parliamentary control. As the final volume was written, Michael Port, one of its two contributors, suggested that there should be a seventh volume covering the period up to the First World War. The issue was raised in the House of Lords, but dismissed.[19] Port later went on to write *Imperial London, Civil Government in London 1851–1915*, effectively the final volume of the history.[20]

We should now turn to the question of money, for this project was an expensive one. Obviously when the question of finding £3,000 for a series of books was raised the Treasury was distinctly unenthusiastic and even Sir Edward Bridges, who had at least some claim to have encouraged Emmerson, was very sceptical but was eventually charmed into providing a budget. Despite the fact that he later admitted it was 'awfully naughty of me to ever agree to this', his final

16 Mark Girouard, 'Summerson, Sir John Newenham', *Oxford Dictionary of National Biography*.

17 *The Functions and Organisation of the Ministry of Public Buildings and Works* (HMSO, n.d.).

18 Sir Harold Emmerson, *The Ministry of Works* (London, 1956); *Daily Telegraph*, 26 October 1956.

19 *Hansard*, vol. 350 cc.581–2 (27 March 1974).

20 Yale University Press, 1995.

approval was given on 15 January 1953. After some legal chicanery the contracts were signed with Colvin a year later.

The details of how the fee structure was agreed were tortuous and reveal Colvin as a shrewd negotiator, pushing the fee up from £4 to £5 per thousand words and even asking if he could be exempted from income tax at one point! Later he negotiated an additional allocation of petrol coupons so he could travel the country and see the sites. He then got the word rate increased to £7 10*s.* per thousand words. And for the whole 30 years of its gestation he kept on top of the complexities of travel, subsistence and incidental expenses. Colvin would have appreciated the archiving of his receipt from the White Cliffs Hotel, Dover, from 10 February 1958 when he stayed in room 207 at a cost of £1 7*s.* 6*d.*

In 1955 the research suddenly went in a new direction. As Howard got to grips with the medieval hunting lodges described in the accounts he realised that not enough survived of any one of them to produce a plan. So he asked the Chief Inspector to excavate the site of King John's Hunting Lodge at Writtle, Essex and to make it part of *The King's Works* research programme. It is easy to forget that archaeology was, in fact, Colvin's first love and history had originally only been a way of pursuing an archaeological career. He had dug before the war at Clarendon Palace and he told the present writer that as an undergraduate he had helped excavate the site of Whitehall Palace, where he presumably first met George Chettle, John Harvey, and other members of the Ancient Monuments Inspectorate. This is an aspect of Colvin's work and of *The History of the King's Works* that has not been adequately understood. *The King's Works* in fact stimulated a massive archaeological research programme. Excavations came fast and furious, a royal house at Clipstone in Nottinghamshire, at Old Sarum, Wiltshire, at the Wakefield Tower at the Tower of London, the vicinity of the Pharos at Dover Castle, and an excavation at Vale Royal which was sponsored by ICI.

While perhaps excavation might have been expected at the medieval sites, what was entirely new was the decision to commission large scale excavation to support the work on the post-medieval buildings. Two large lost palaces, Oatlands in Weybridge and Greenwich Palace, were subject to major investigations. While at three extant structures, Hampton Court, the Banqueting House, Whitehall, and Camber Castle there were extensive investigations too.

Biggest of all was Nonsuch. The excavation of Nonsuch in fact started as a private venture by Captain A. W. G. Lowther, a prominent member of the Surrey Archaeological Society. Colvin was initially in touch with him in 1955 but nothing came of it and it was in 1957 that Martin Biddle suggested that an excavation would reveal more or less the whole plan. Biddle had been employed by the ministry as an assistant Inspector and though he had left for university life still had a contract to write much of the Tudor material. With the support of Arnold Taylor and Sir John Summerson, Biddle and his team excavated the site of the main palace at Nonsuch in 1959.

In parallel with these excavations came the huge and expensive task of undertaking new surveys of the major sites. There was no modern survey of the whole of Dover castle and even the Inspectorate baulked at the cost of this. But it was done as were new surveys of dozens of other sites covered by the history. Colvin then asked for seven of these to be printed at large scale, 4ft by 3ft. And moreover he wanted them coloured like the phase plans in the back of the Ministry of Works Blue Guides.

These hugely ambitious plans and many others were all undertaken by the Ancient Monuments Drawing Office, latterly under the leadership of the late Alan Cook. The drawing office made a huge contribution to *The Kings Works* and had its own series of parallel meetings with Colvin at which the plans would be discussed in detail.

Of course historians had used archaeological excavations and large scale survey to help support their enquiries before. W. H. St John Hope being perhaps one of the most successful,[21] but what took place for the Kings Works was unprecedented then and has never been repeated in this country – a systematic series of major archaeological excavations undertaken to inform a big narrative history. Clearly Colvin was the intellectual impresario behind this but the methodology firmly belonged to the Ancient Monuments Inspectorate. Well before the war inspectors were linking what they had found in the Public Records Office with their own excavations. Indeed the excavations at Whitehall in which Colvin had participated as a youth were pioneering in this respect. Arnold Taylor was a key figure because he was the leading senior exponent of this approach. In this way although *The King's Works* was a personal achievement for Howard it was also the crowning achievement of the old Inspectorate of Ancient Monuments, embodying a generation of research and experience. In the case of the Ministry's Blue Guides quite literally, for these were examined by Colvin and absorbed into the text. But there was a terrible weakness. In its review of the first two volumes of *The King's Works* in the *Times Literary Supplement* in 1964 it was noted that few of the excavations mentioned in the text had been written up.[22] Colvin thought this a fair criticism but not the fault of *The King's Works*, rather the fault of the Inspectorate. He was right as this whole period was dogged by the inability of inspectors to write up their excavations.

[21] A. H. Thompson, 'Hope, Sir William Henry St. John', *Oxford Dictionary of National Biography*.

[22] *Times Literary Supplement*, 16 January 1964, p. 44.

The King's Works was written in a Whitehall which was very different from today after the creation of QUANGOs fragmented the sense of being part of a single governmental machine. The Ordnance Survey, the British Museum, and the Government Art Collection were all drawn in, the Paris Embassy obtained a plan of Falaise and the Air Ministry provided air photographs of Calais. Original manuscripts relating to royal building were hunted down, funds raised and they were bought for public collections. This is a lost world, as lost as the gentle pursuits of the Ministry of Works Inspectors.

So what did *The History of the King's Works* do for us? Most reviews of the volumes were favourable and marvelled at the huge amount of new information available.[23] Famously, in the pages of *Architectural History*, the late Andor Gomme questioned the right of *The Kings Works* to be called a history and suggested that the achievement was the creation of a 'spectacularly laid out research file'.[24] Colvin was not much pleased by this and wrote to Joe Crook 'I do not like Andor Gomme's style of reviewing, and I thought this specimen of it rather unpleasant in tone as usual. I rather wish he would confine himself to Eng. Lit. where he is, I am told, equally offensive but perhaps better qualified'.[25]

The King's Works was important for two reasons. The first is an institutional one. While it is impossible to make any direct links between the methodology of *The Kings Works* and the daily practice of the Inspectorate, there is no doubt that it contributed to the decisive shift away from the Inspectorate being dominated by architects and archaeologists and the emergence of a new breed of architectural historian. Even in the 1950s the majority of investigators and many Inspectors had been architects and there is a sense in which the Office of Works was staffed by architects consumed by the dying embers of the gothic revival. John Harvey, perhaps, could be seen in this category, with his view of Old England that was almost Puginesque. Summerson too (who had been employed by the Ministry of Works after the War) epitomised this type of approach, but Arnold Taylor and Colvin were something else entirely and brought a rigour and discipline to the work of the Inspectorate that had not been there before.

But what about the content of the volumes? Andor Gomme was right in a sense; *The King's Works* is a huge research file, because most scholars use it not for its administrative history but because it is the way in to understanding some of the most important buildings in English architectural history. But the administrative history is important too because it demonstrates the absolute

23 *Society of Architectural Historians Newsletter* 38 (1970), pp. 285–287; *English Historical Review* 80 (1965), pp. 553–556.

24 Andor Gomme, 'History, chronicle or research file?', *Architectural History* 29 (1986), pp. 197–203.

25 J. M. Crook, Pers. comm.

centrality of the Office of Works to English architectural practice. It is easy to forget that in the Middle Ages the English crown was more often than not the leading architectural patron; Henry III, Edward III, the extraordinary works of piety of Henry VI – completed and rivalled by those of Edward IV, Henry VII, and only completed by Henry VIII – Henry VIII's megalomaniac domestic and military building campaigns, William III's massive construction programme, George III's palaces and civil building, and of course George IV's personal architectural orgy. The history of English architecture cannot be written without these. The second point *The King's Works* demonstrates without question is the central importance of the Office of Works in the training of architectural designers and the transmission of architectural ideas. During the seventeenth and eighteenth centuries it was where the opportunities were and, as Colvin himself pointed out, it was the unacknowledged substitute for a royal academy of architecture such as Colbert had established in France. Understanding the mechanisms of the Office of Works is essential for unravelling the process of design at the heart of English architecture.

In the end *The History of the King's Works* was five volumes, not three, with 3,713 pages, 232 plates, 227 figures, and seven portfolio plans. The official cost rose to £11,150 but this was a fraction of the real cost as the resources of the Inspectorate were never added in. This was monumental history in every sense of the word and it laid the foundations for the modern understanding of English architecture.

Chapter Nine

ARCHITECTURAL HISTORY AT OXFORD: PAST AND FUTURE

J. Mordaunt Crook

Oxford may never have had a Professor of Architectural History – Oxford never has had a Professor of Architectural History – but the University once had a Regius Professor of Modern History who was – among many other things – an architectural historian. His name was Edward Augustus Freeman. He did not invent the term 'Architectural History'. That privilege is reserved for the great Robert Willis of Cambridge.[1] Willis's trump card was the linking of documentation with archaeological explanation. He was a master of manuscript evidence and at the same time a master of structural analysis. But he was not much interested in architecture as a conceptual formula. He resigned from the Cambridge Camden Society in 1841 because he thought it had gone too far beyond archaeology: it was becoming an engine of polemical theology. By contrast, Freeman was concerned above all with context, with cultural context. In 1856 he resigned from the Archaeological Institute precisely because it excluded 'philosophical and religious views'.[2] And in 1855, in the Holywell Music Room in Oxford, he nailed his colours to the mast in a very characteristic speech. 'Architecture', he announced, is 'the highest of the arts.' Because architecture is 'history speaking'. Total history; speaking 'in stones and bricks'.[3] Freeman regarded buildings as themselves cultural constructs. Architectural study was to him simply 'a branch of history'; ultimately a branch of the history of ideas.[4] He

1 W. R. W. Stephens, ed., *Life and Letters of Edward A. Freeman* (2 vols., London, 1895), vol. ii, pp. 27–9. Willis used this term as early as 1845 in his *Architectural History of Canterbury Cathedral.* 'There have been few minds of greater power ... than the mind of Professor Willis' (Freeman, *The Methods of Historical Study* [London, 1886], pp. 235–6). 'As a lecturer he was simply perfect ... The phrase 'architectural history' was his own invention. Here was the written record: there were the stones of which the record spoke. Each in his hands explained the other' ([E. A. Freeman], 'Professor Robert Willis', *Saturday Review* xxxix [1875], p. 341.)

2 Stephens, *Freeman*, i, pp. 96-7, Freeman to J. L. Patterson: 7 Sept. 1846.

3 *Ecclesiologist,* xvi, ns xiii (1855), p. 249.

4 Architecture's 'true place is as a branch ... of history. Buildings are the most visibly permanent things which men leave behind them, and to know how men built at any given age is as natural a part of the history of that age as to know how they fought or legislated ... the succession of styles in architecture cannot be understood in all its fullness, except by one who is really an historian' (Bod. MS. Dep. c 590, f 489, Freeman to J. H. Parker: 12 June 1860).

would certainly have seen the point of Collingwood's dictum: 'All history is the history of thought'.[5]

Now in that speech of 1855 Freeman was addressing the Oxford Architectural Society. Founded in 1839 – a few weeks before the Cambridge Camden Society – it was originally called the Oxford Society for the Promotion of Gothic Architecture. The fact that its name was changed to a more generalised form indicates its emancipation from religious and chronological restrictions. It refused to be identified, for example, with the Oxford Movement. Cardinal Newman called their headquarters 'the only neutral ground in Oxford'.[6] Young Ruskin was a member, though he had little or nothing in common with its leading lights, E. A. Freeman and J. H. Parker.[7] The Society rented space in Holywell Street – in the oldest public Music Room in Europe – from 1845 to 1860.[8] And there it built up a library, and a collection of models, fragments, and drawings. From 1861 it met in the Clarendon Building, then in the Ashmolean, eventually calling itself by an even wider title: 'The Oxford Architectural and Historical Society'.[9] As such it became a pressure group for the creation of a broadly-based History Faculty in the University, encompassing the study of all aspects of historical evidence, not least the study of history's physical manifestation in architectural form: what the mid-Victorians called Architectural Archaeology.[10]

It is not my purpose here to tell the story of the OAHS. But I like to think that the breadth of its approach – the buildings of the past as history in four dimensions (the fourth being the dimension of time) – is not without relevance today. Freeman's emphasis on architectural context – political, religious, economic, intellectual context – helps to make possible, for example, an explanation of one key aspect of the Victorian mind: its attitude to the medieval past. In

5 R. G. Collingwood, *The Idea of History* (Oxford, 1946), pp. 115, 282.

6 Quoted in S. L. Ollard, 'The Oxford Architectural and Historical Society and the Oxford Movement', *Oxoniensia* 5 (1940), pp. 146–60. For membership lists see W. A. Pantin, 'The Oxford Architectural and Historical Society', *Oxoniensia* 4 (1939), pp. 174–94.

7 For Parker's obituaries, see *Builder* xlvi (1884), pp. 189, 211 and *Building News* xlvi (1884), pp. 225–6. For Freeman's obituary, see *Building News* lxii (1892), p. 424.

8 Built in 1742, described as 'The Temple of Harmony' in *The Student, or Oxford and Cambridge Monthly Miscellany* ii (1751), pp. 197, 372, cited in Christopher Wordsworth, *Social Life at the English Universities in the 18th Century* (Cambridge, 1874), p. 201. See also Falconer Madan, *Oxford Outside the Guidebooks* (Oxford, 1923), p. 96.

9 *Ecclesiologist* xxii, ns xix (1861), pp. 48, 267, 269. For the Society's evolution, see David Prout, '"The Oxford Society for Promoting the Study of Gothic Architecture" and "The Oxford Architectural Society", 1839–1860', *Oxoniensia* 54 (1989), pp. 379–91.

10 In Acland's words, 'there ought to be a Professor of Art [at Oxford], and until there should be, the [Oxford Architectural] Society should do a professor's work' (*Ecclesiologist* xvii, ns xiii [1856], p. 69). Similarly, James Parker (ibid., xviii, ns xiv [1857], p. 122), and J. H. Parker (ibid xx, ns xvii [1859], pp. 55–6).

Oxford more than anywhere the Victorians could not escape the Middle Ages. The medieval world supplied a prism through which they could view their own time: a prism and a mirror too. A century later, the very architecture the Victorians created supplies us with just such a prism, but this time to explain what G. M. Young called the 'anfractuosities' of the Victorian mind itself.[11]

* * *

Now let's see how this group of Oxford Victorians – Freeman in particular – can help us solve a few of our present discontents. I shall begin by being purposely provocative. Architectural history in England, as my own generation was able to practise it forty years ago, is now over. It has become logistically impossible; and it has become methodologically redundant. Take the logistics first. From the 1960s to the 1990s – apart from short periods at Oxford and Cambridge – I was chiefly based at London University, at Bedford College in Regent's Park. By modern standards, the teaching load was tolerable, the administrative burden was negligible, and the salary was adequate. In money of the 1960s my Lecturer's stipend began symbolically at £1485. There were no sabbaticals. But I had time to do research. And in the 1960s the conditions were very favourable. Just a stroll away from Regent's Park was the RIBA Drawings Collection, the RIBA Early Works Library, and the RIBA periodicals collection. All at 66 Portland Place, all free of charge, and all entirely open access. There was even a subsidised lunch. Another short stroll away was the National Monuments Record in Savile Row: immediate open access, every weekday, to thousands of photographic files. From there it was only a short walk to the British Museum: the Round Reading Room, the Manuscripts Room, the Print Room, the Map Room, the State Paper Room – miraculously open until 9 pm most nights, and all in the same Bloomsbury complex. Across the road was the Architectural Association, with its open lectures and ever-open bar; and Birkbeck College, where Summerson and Pevsner used to lecture in the evening – though not on the same evening. Across another road was the Institute of Historical Research, with its welcoming tea, headquarters of the Victoria County History and the History of Parliament. The unique library of the Warburg Institute, with its polymathic personnel, was a matter of yards away. And a short stroll from all of these was the Soane Museum in Lincoln's Inn Fields; the Public Record Office in Chancery Lane; and the Probate Office in Somerset House. The working conditions in many of these institutions might be Victorian – they were Victorian – but they were extraordinarily accessible. To crown it all, the hospitable headquarters of *Country Life* were still housed in a Lutyens building in Covent Garden. Happy days. I could – and very often did – work in

[11] G. M. Young, *Portrait of an Age* (1936), ed. G. Kitson Clark (Oxford, 1977), p. 125.

half a dozen of these world-class centres of research in any one day, day and night in fact, free of charge. So, in the 1960s and 1970s I was able to write *The King's Works*, *Eastlake*, *The British Museum*, *The Greek Revival,* and *William Burges*; and to organise the architectural section of the Neo-classical exhibition, and the two Burges centenary exhibitions in London and Cardiff. Thanks to the backing of Sir Ernst Gombrich in 1967, I was able to introduce a new Optional Subject on the Gothic Revival in the London University History and History of Art syllabus. And by 1981 I could call myself England's first Professor of Architectural History.[12]

A generation later, all is changed. I speak here, again, of England only. Scotland handles these things rather better. Bedford College has gone to Egham. The RIBA drawings have gone, via Portman Square, to South Kensington (thus losing their temporary partnership with the Courtauld Institute). That, incidentally, was where I held the first Society of Architectural Historians one-day symposium in 1971. The National Monuments Record has now gone to Swindon; its Welsh section has gone to Aberystwyth. The British Museum's resources have been divided: large parts have gone to the British Library at St Pancras. The PRO has gone to Kew; the Probate Office to somewhere in North London; *Country Life* to somewhere near the Isle of Dogs. In curatorial terms, accessibility has become less important than security and economy. And this fragmentation of resources has involved not only material resources but, crucially, the interpersonal contacts – the people – that went with them. This informal community of scholars[13] has not been replicated (as many assumed it would be) by the magic of the internet. Nor by cheaper reproduction fees. Certainly not by easier communications. Country house snooping is now ruled out by security devices; and road travel is an ordeal. Try getting from Cambridge to Swindon. Try getting from Oxford to Aberystwyth. Try getting from anywhere outside London to Kew and back again in a day. Try ordering Parliamentary Papers – not open access but item by item – at St Pancras. Try comparing prints with printed books at the British Library. Try comparing drawings with early printed works at the V. and A. Writing the *King's Works* – within the time-span we achieved – would now be quite impossible. Even if we were to write it, publishing it on the lavish scale of those HMSO volumes – with a veritable team of draughtsmen on tap, preparing those amazing plans – would now be seriously impossible. And – if only on insurance grounds – there will never again be an exhibition like *The Age of Neo-Classicism*. So much for logistics.

[12] J. Mordaunt Crook 'Architecture and History' (Inaugural Lecture, 1983), *Architectural History* 27 (1984), pp. 558–78.

[13] Colvin evokes the advantages of this earlier world in 'Architectural History and its Records', in *Archives* 2 (1955), pp. 300–311.

Now for the methodological side of things. This is trickier to argue. But I've rather come to the conclusion that much of the work we did in those days is now methodologically redundant. The definitive RIBA Drawings catalogue (1969 onwards), masterminded by John Harris, is unlikely ever to be re-catalogued. Colvin's *Dictionary* can only be done once. It can be revised. He famously revised it himself, three times. But in the future successive revisers will rapidly run into the law of diminishing returns. The same is true of Pevsner. Those invaluable volumes – I speak again of England – are still being revised; but their revision is coming to an end. They need not be written three times over. As for *The King's Works*, it may be extended – I hope it will be extended – but it cannot be written again. And many architectural monographs need never be repeated – though I have to admit that a new edition of *Burges* is now out. In some ways, this process of change is epitomised in the winding down of the RCHM volumes, and even in the slow completion of the *Survey of London*. We have come to the end of a phase; a truly heroic phase, in architectural history. It's over. But there are compensations. We are now free: free to do different things. Let's explore some of the possibilities.

Firstly, we have to recognise that we have lived through a significant professional change, stemming from the growth of the conservation movement. In the 1980s and 1990s this supplied career opportunities for an increasing number of graduates. But it also had its drawbacks. It involved politicising the preservation process and narrowing research in the direction of listed documentation. Of course I simplify for the purposes of argument. But I suspect that the sudden expansion of this sector will soon come to be seen as a single-generation phenomenon. It will continue, but at a lesser level of production; dependent in part on the property market. Secondly, and more promisingly from a conceptual point of view, there has been since the 1970s a broadening of architectural studies at university level to include a variety of cognate disciplines: history in all its facets – political, economic, administrative, local; along with geography – human and physical, landscape design, town planning, and social policy; as well as, for example, aesthetics, ecology, and cultural studies. So we are already in a post-Colvinian era.

Let me quote to you one comment. He

> found a mass of half-knowledge, overgrown with picturesque and stubborn weeds. This ground he ... not only cleared, but in his own inimitable, lapidary way ... covered with a structure of facts as hard and certain as granite. On his ground [and] in his own manner, nothing else remains to be done.

Well, I've cheated there. That was written in 1939; not about Colvin, but about one economic historian (J. H. Clapham) by another (M. M. Postan).[14] Still the analogy holds true. 'On his ground [and] in his own manner, nothing else remains to be done ...'. But the ground has changed; still more the manner. Because the idea of history ever changes; and architectural history cannot escape that process.

The results of this twenty-first-century transformation have been academically multifarious. Architectural history has been diversified and, in parallel, the humanities in general have been re-focused: away from the abstractions of literary theory – thank goodness – and towards the specificity of material form. Architectural history – and here I speak as a Warburg affiliate: I've always believed, with Fritz Saxl, that 'art history is just a piece of history' – architectural history is now exactly where it should be: part of the endless complexity of cultural history; at the very heart of the history of ideas.[15] And its objectivity may now even be improved by emancipation from the constraints of preservation politics. The new globalisation has certainly speeded up intellectual interchange. Naming names is invidious. But I think I can safely say that among the next generation, geographers are re-writing the architecture of the eighteenth-century landscape and the nineteenth-century town; art historians are re-thinking the symbolism of medieval royal and ecclesiastical buildings; architectural historians are re-interpreting the eclecticism of Victorian imperial imagery; economic historians are re-valuing the country house as an index of consumption; and social historians are re-constituting the language of the eighteenth-century domestic interior.

The study of architectural history in England can never be the same as it was forty years ago. Post Colvin, its future has to be interpretive and contextual rather than documentary or archaeological. Our field of action has widened immeasurably. And this involves, intellectually speaking, taking risks. By training and by temperament, Colvin was risk-averse. As he once reminded me, 'the extirpation of error [is] always more important than additional information'.[16] He was ultimately a product of the Manchester School of History. His teacher was V. H. Galbraith, who was taught by T. F. Tout (founder of the Manchester School), who in turn was taught by the immortal Stubbs. So, academically speaking, Colvin was Stubbs's great grandson. Now this tradition reverenced, above all, medieval constitutional and administrative archives. Hence *The King's Works*. The Manchester School was born in the PRO and died in the Rylands Library. By the 1940s its methods had been refined into an ideal of almost

[14] Quoted in N. B. Harte, ed., *The Study of Economic History: collected inaugural lectures 1893–1970* (London, 1971), p. 129.

[15] For general discussions, see *The Listener* xlviii (1952), pp. 715–16, 761–2 and *Burlington Magazine*, Feb. to March 1949.

[16] Colvin to J.M.C.: 7 March 2004.

bloodless professionalism. Its technique, wrote Herbert Butterfield in the 1930s, 'is essentially a negative thing ... a gigantic science of caution, a colossal elimination of ... self'.[17] As the redoubtable K. B. McFarlane put it, a successful 'article has damn well got to leave [its readers] with no alternative [but agreement]'. His aim was to close down debate, not open up a dialogue. No wonder other scholars went in awe of him. But even McFarlane found the Colvinian manner 'dry'.[18] Anyway, it was such attitudes as these that the next generation of historians, in the later 1950s, began to reject. '*Manchesterismus*', exploded Trevor-Roper in 1957 in a letter to Wallace Notestein; '*Manchesterismus* has killed [the writing of history]: the Manchester medievalism of Tout and Tait, Davis and Powicke, Jacob and Galbraith, and that brood of clerically-minded hacks ... [all] mere boring antiquarians ... What we need is a new spirit – the spirit of Pirenne or Bloch, Febvre or Braudel ... [Even] Namierism has degenerated ... into the cult of *minutiae*'.[19] The first fruits of Trevor-Roper's purge was felt – as I remember well – in the choice of set books for History Prelims in 1955–56: not de Tocqueville and the Venerable Bede but Michelet and Erasmus. On Erasmus we were lucky enough to be taught by the future Sir John Hale – a future contributor to *The King's Works* – soon to leave Oxford, alas, first for a chair in History, then for a chair in Art History, and finally for a chair in Italian. During the later 1960s and early 1970s, the pace of change began to quicken, even in Oxford. Compulsory Constitutional Documents were abolished, along with the compulsory grand sweep of English History. The ghost of Stubbs had been banished: and with it went the core rationale of the Oxford History syllabus.[20] One of the signs of this on-going revolution was the inclusion in the new syllabus of Colvin's Architectural History Special Subject.

Generalising from one's own experience can be delusional. But I like to think that my own work during this transitional phase was not entirely random. During the 1980s and 1990s, with *The Dilemma of Style* and *The Architect's Secret*, I began to move away from architectural history as architectural biography and archaeological documentation. I began to think, more and more, of architecture

17 Quoted in Michael Bentley, *Modernizing England's Past: English historiography in the age of modernism, 1870–1970* (Cambridge, 2005), p. 201.

18 K. B. McFarlane, *Letters to Friends 1940–60*, ed. G. L. Harriss (Oxford 1997), pp. 68, 224: to Norman Scarfe 1949.

19 To Wallace Notestein 1957. Quoted in Bentley *Modernizing England's Past*, p. 231.

20 In his Chichele Inaugural (1961), R. W. Southern 'sounded the death knell of the Pipe Roll' (Alexander Murray, 'R. W. Southern', in *Proceedings of the British Academy* 120 [2003], p. 433). 'English medieval history, as a teaching subject, has lost a discipline and has not found a role' (David Knowles, in *Transactions of the Royal Historical Society*, 5th ser. 19 [1969], p. 157).

as a cultural phenomenon; to use the modern jargon, as a semiotic code: the handwriting of the age. We build our houses in our own image. With *The Rise of the Nouveaux Riches*, I came to see buildings increasingly from this perspective, in terms of social imagery; in that particular case as the interrelationship of style and status. And with *Brasenose: the Biography of an Oxford College* I tried to explain a single institution in a single building – as I had done with *The British Museum* nearly forty years before – as the setting for an on-going social narrative; exemplar of that encompassing framework within which we all live and move and have our being.

* * *

Now back to Edward Freeman, the second best Professor of Architectural History Oxford never had. He has something to teach us in all of this. Between the 1840s and the 1880s Freeman played a significant part – not always a constructive part, but a significant part – in the creation of a new university discipline: the Oxford School of Modern History. Modern history at Oxford – as distinct from Ancient History – began to be taught in 1850, in conjunction with Law, as a postscript to Classical Greats. Law and History together became a separate school in 1864. History achieved its own independence in 1872. Freeman was not exactly happy about this. History and Law, he complained, go together about as well as 'Law and Hydrostatics, or ... Phlebotomy and Modern History'. And, anyway, the chronology of a distinct 'Modern History', he thought, will always be an '*ignis fatuus*': 'Why separate modern history from ancient?' he asked in 1849.[21] The classicists had an answer: because ancient history belonged with Greek and Latin. And the pedagogic processes of classical teaching – the famous Oxford gobbet – survived (via the study of Constitutional Documents) to dominate the Modern History syllabus at Oxford until the 1970s. Nor was Freeman any more successful in arguing for the abolition of 1066 as in any sense a dividing line. Still, he acted as examiner on a number of occasions, notably in 1857-58 when he incurred the wrath of the Protestant Alliance by adding 'a Romish writer' – John Lingard – to the list of recommended books.[22] When he returned to Oxford full time as Regius Professor in 1884, he found the architecture of the city much changed but the

21 [Freeman], *The Guardian*, Feb. 1849; *Thoughts on the Study of History with reference to the proposed changes in the public examination* (Oxford, 1849; 2nd edn. with *Postscript on the Revised Form of the New Statute*, 1849); *Thoughts on the Third Form of the New Examination Statute* (Oxford, 1850); Evidence to the First Oxford University Commission, *Parliamentary Papers* 1852, XXII, Appendix, 136–42; *Suggestions with Regard to Certain Proposed Alterations in the University ... of Oxford* (Committee of the Tutors' Association, Paper xii, 1854), p. 140.

22 Stephens, *Freeman* vol. i, pp. 216–19; [Freeman], 'Historical Study at Oxford', *British Quarterly Review,* March 1859 and *Bentley's Quarterly Review* i (1859), pp. 828–300.

institutional power of the college tutors – 'the crammers' as he called them – still invincible.[23]

It was Freeman's belief all along that this newly formed Oxford curriculum should indeed include the study of architectural history, but 'situated directly as a branch of history, with constant references to the creeds, the feelings, and the laws of the times and places where successive architectural styles arose'. Otherwise, he believed, the subject would just lapse into antiquarianism; and become 'a mere matter of curiosity ... [like] the collection of postage-stamps'.[24] That was in 1871. 'As a branch of history', he repeated in 1876, the history of architecture is well 'worthy of [a] place alongside the history of law and of language'.[25] But not as a subject on its own. Architectural history, he believed should fight for its space at Oxford as an integral part of what he called 'the unity of history'. Interestingly, in 1952 that was rather Pevsner's view of the teaching of art history at Oxford and Cambridge.[26] That tradition – a general education in the humanities – is far too easy to despise. To dismiss Kenneth Clark and John Pope-Hennessy; or H. Avray Tipping and Christopher Hussey, for example, as mere Oxford amateurs because they read History not Art History, would be very foolish. Even Tipping – perhaps a marginal case – was no lightweight: in 1878, he took a First in Modern History when such things were very rare; and his chief examiner was Stubbs.[27]

Freeman died in 1892, a disappointed man. The influence of 'cribmonger Jowett and that lot', as he called them, had proved too much for him.[28] But the arguments in which he was involved still had a long way to run. The story of the abortive attempts to establish history of art and architecture at Oxford is indeed a long and sorry one. In 2004 Sir John Boardman called it, in print, a tale of 'obstruction, ignorance, sheer jealousy [and] arrogance'.[29] Let's look for a

23 Freeman's Inaugural, 'The Office of Historical Professor', was reprinted in his *Methods of Historical Study*.

24 Freeman, 'Address to the Historical Section [of the R.A.I.] at Cardiff', *Archaeological Journal* xxviii (1871), p. 178.

25 Freeman, *The History of the Norman Conquest, Its Causes and Results* (5 vols., London, 1867-76), vol. v, p. viii. See also *Saturday Review* xxxvii (1874), pp. 437–8.

26 Nikolaus Pevsner, 'Reflections on Not Teaching Art History', and Ellis Waterhouse, 'Art as a "Piece of History"', *The Listener* xlviii (1952), pp. 715–16 and 761–2.

27 Christopher Hussey, 'Gardener and Antiquary' [H. Avray Tipping], *Country Life* lxxiv (1933), pp. 567–8; J. Mordaunt Crook, 'Christopher Hussey: a bibliographical tribute', *Architectural History* 13 (1970), pp. 5–29. Tipping – born at Avray, near Paris – succeeded Charles Latham, who took his own photographs. Between 1917 and 1957 *Country Life's* chief photographer was A. E. Henson (d. 1972). See *Country Life*, 20 Jan. 1972, p. 150 (A. S. Oswald). Among those listed with Tipping in the brief 1878 class list was Freeman's nemesis, J. H. Round.

28 Freeman to Bryce, c. 1886 (Bodl. MS. Bryce 6, fs 90–92).

29 *Oxford Magazine* 8th week, Michaelmas term, 2004, p. 13; summarizing Donna Kurtz, ed.,

moment at some of these failures.

As early as 1843 Richard Greswell of Worcester College campaigned for nothing less than an Oxford institute of art studies, complete with a Chair in Art Theory.[30] There was a good deal of such thinking in the air in the 1840s. 'Why', asked G. H. Lewes in 1842; 'why is there no Professor of Aesthetics at Oxford?'[31] Why indeed. In 1852 the first Parliamentary Commission to reform the University recommended the establishment of a Lectureship in Art, 'especially that of Greece', to be linked to the Ashmolean.[32] That was a beginning, but no more than that. In 1856 the Revd. George Butler of Exeter College – a kinsman of the future Lady Colvin – called for the introduction of at least some form of art-historical teaching in Oxford.[33] Again nothing came of it.

In 1861 in a lecture to the OAHS,[34] and again in 1877 in a letter to the second Parliamentary Commission,[35] Freeman's old ally J. H. Parker produced powerful pleas for the establishment of what he called archaeological studies at Oxford. Parker's letter of 1877, belatedly printed in 1881, presented a detailed programme largely based at the Ashmolean, for a full-scale school of teaching and research: a Professor, a Reader, and a Lecturer teaching Greek, Roman, and Medieval Architecture, as well as Sculpture and Painting. And a Medieval Museum as well, to be housed in a chantry priest's house opposite St Michael's church. At the same time Montagu Burrows was campaigning, in effect, for a Department of Architectural Archaeology, but attached to Modern History rather than to the Ashmolean. H. W. Acland thought its headquarters should be in the Radcliffe Camera. But the Hebdomadel Council backed Jowett's rival scheme for a chair of 'Classical Archaeology and Art'.[36] At the same time, Ruskin was campaigning in vain for expanded facilities for what would one day be the Ruskin School of Drawing.[37] Eventually, in 1918 a Committee for the Fine Arts was appointed to look after the Slade Professors and the Ruskin School. It lingered on for half a century and more, but without much institutional effect. In 1923 and 1928 there were campaigns for improved art teaching at Oxford, and for a professional

---

'The Study of Art at Oxford before 1955', in eadem, *Reception of Classical Art, an Introduction* (Oxford, 2004).

30 BL. ADD. MSS. 40537, fs 59–67 and 44181 (correspondence with Gladstone).

31 J. Mordaunt Crook, *The Architect's Secret* (London, 2003), pp. 149, 191.

32 First Oxford University Commission, *Parliamentary Papers* 1852, XXII, 102, 123.

33 *Oxford Essays* (Oxford, 1856), pp. 188–92.

34 *Ecclesiologist* xxii, ns xix (1861), pp. 161, 50–51.

35 Selborne Commission, *Parliamentary Papers* 1881, LVI, 376–7: letter of 20 Dec. 1877 (not indexed).

36 Ibid., 52, 195, 317.

37 Ibid., 395. Ruskin predicted that his post would become a sinecure unless it was attached to an art history department (*The Architect* xi [1874], p. 351).

School of Architecture. Once again, nothing happened, at least within the University itself.[38] And worse was to come. Between 1928 and 1936 Oxford missed its chance to provide a home for both the Courtauld Institute and the Warburg Institute. We could have had both. And in the next generation we could have had Kelmscott and Harold Acton's La Pietra, Florence, as well. Physicists tell us that inertia is the greatest force of all. But it was darker than that. All the way through, it was the entrenched opposition of the college tutors – classicists and historians – that lay at the root of the problem. Cambridge, with its stronger Faculty tradition, never had the same trouble. Jowett's comment on Ruskin's first Slade Lecture has echoed down the years: 'Very poor taste, very poor taste'. As for Walter Pater, lecturing at Brasenose for thirty years, Jowett regarded him as a mere 'demoralizing moralizer'.[39] This tradition of suspicion and hostility continued even into the 1980s. When Boardman attempted to establish an MSt. in the Classical Tradition in Art, he was given very short shrift.

* * *

Back to Colvin. When he arrived at St John's in 1948, architectural history at Oxford existed only in the agreeable shape of Billy Pantin of Oriel, Lecturer in Medieval Archaeology and History. Pantin belonged to a persistent Oxford tradition of medieval topography descending ultimately from Anthony Wood. But of post-medieval architectural history in the University at that time there was nothing. The Slade lectures of 1933-36 by Goodhart-Rendel were already a fading memory.[40] Nor was art history – apart from classical archaeology – much better represented. But in 1949 T. S. R. Boase – previously first director of the Courtauld, then President of Magdalen – set up an ambitious new project: *The Oxford History of English Art*. Of its eleven volumes, Boase wrote two himself: one on the Saxons and one on the Victorians. The series is by no means undistinguished. But its essentially Oxford origins are only too obvious: as the preface explained, it aimed to integrate the history of art and architecture 'as part of the general history of England'.[41]

That was not calculated to please art historians outside the Oxford orbit. Hence the greater impact of Pevsner's rival Pelican History of Art Series. Attempts to reverse Oxford's apparent parochialism proved difficult to achieve. In 1945 a

[38] *Oxford Magazine*, 25 Jan. 1923, pp. 158–61, 174, 177–8 (H. C. Corlette); R. Gleadhowe, 'Oxford University and the Fine Arts', *RIBA Journal* xxxv (1928), pp. 636–40, 676–79. For the origins of the Oxford School of Architecture, later part of Oxford Brookes University, see *Oxford School of Architecture: the first 70 years* (Oxford, 1997).

[39] For this episode, see J. Mordaunt Crook, *Brasenose: the biography of an Oxford college* (Oxford, 2008), p. 281.

[40] H. S. Goodhart-Rendel, *English Architecture Since the Regency* (London, 1953).

[41] Introduction to Joan Evans, *English Art 1307–1461* (Oxford, 1949), p. v.

learned Viennese refugee named Otto Pächt had been appointed to an Oxford Lectureship in the History of Medieval Art. But hardly anyone came to his lectures on incunabula; and over a period of twenty years he had just two postgraduate pupils. Not until 1955 did Oxford elect its first established Professor in the History of Art: Edgar Wind.[42] Now Wind's lectures filled the Playhouse, as did Kenneth Clark's Slade Lectures; but their subjects remained firmly excluded from the Examination Schools. Ellis Waterhouse predicted that there would be no art history at Oxford until it could be classified as a lost cause. It was not until the late 1960s, under Wind's successor Francis Haskell, that the Oxford Modern History syllabus incorporated a Special Subject in French nineteenth-century art criticism. But Haskell, like Wind – and unlike Michael Jaffé at Cambridge – was not interested in expanding his teaching empire to exploit, for example, the post-classical resources of the Ashmolean. Oxford's loss turned out to be Cambridge's gain. It was not until 2004 – 50 years after its first established art historical chair, 135 years after Ruskin's appointment as its first Slade Professor – that Oxford set up a separate Honour School in the History of Art. Meanwhile Pächt, who had been passed over in favour of Wind, returned to Vienna in 1963, leaving vacant the Readership to which he had been appointed just one year previously. Colvin – at that point still a teaching Fellow in medieval history – was nominated in his place. Up to that date the only instruction available in, for example, Baroque or Palladian architecture had been Summerson's Slade Lectures of 1958–59.

As Reader in Architectural History, Colvin was able at last in 1965 to establish his own Special Subject: 'English Architectural History, 1660–1720'. The training of a new species of scholar had begun. At a different time, and in different hands, this newly installed discipline might well have supplied a pedagogic bridge between the conceptual framework of Continental art theory and the empirical traditions of English historiography. It was not to be. Set texts and gobbets remained. And Colvin continued in strictly empirical mode. He belonged to an earlier discipline altogether: the school of William Camden and Richard Gough. That was his inheritance; and he would, as he once told me, 'stick to his last'. Meanwhile the Slade Lectures remained essentially 'off syllabus'; as with my own Slade Lectures of 1979–80, and my Waynflete Lectures of 1984–85. If Colvin ever entertained the slightest doubt about all this, it was surely blanked out by those two mighty projects which dominated his thinking, the *Dictionary* and *The King's Works*.

42 "I fear he is a humbug" (Trevor-Roper to Bernard Berezan). Maurice Brown thought him "a spell-binder", but harmless. "There is no school of Art History in the University which he can lead into ever by his ignorance: he will be but a professor lecturing in the void to susceptible femmes du monde" (quoted in S. Harris, *Nikolaus Pevsner* (London, 2011), p. 679.

As late as 1981, Colvin was still hoping that an established Lectureship in Architectural History might be set up – 'in, say, 20 years' time' he told me – at either London or Oxford University.[43] Alas, he had little taste for academic politics. When he retired in 1987, his Readership in Architectural History was not renewed. Nor was my own personal chair in Architectural History when I retired from London University in the year 2000.

The fact that Colvin never became a Professor deprived us of one key statement: an Inaugural Lecture, setting out the principles by which the pursuit of architectural history might be governed. My guess is that it would have been a pretty Broad Church document, allowing for complementary approaches from historians, from architects, and from art historians. For there will always be a need for architect-historians or engineer-historians to explain how a building operates in structural and spatial terms, as well as a need for art and architectural historians to explain the cultural origins of that same building in contextual terms.[44] In the same way, there will always be a need for historians of economics to compare the ideas of Ricardo and Keynes, as well as economic historians to explain the dynamics of industrial and post-industrial society. Territorial disputes between schools of architecture, faculties of history, and departments of art history – competing for the soul of architectural history – rather miss the point. It's really just a question of emphasis.

* * *

So where do we stand today? At the risk of sounding too much like a valedictory lecturer, here are a few suggestions. The study of history in general has benefited hugely from the recent diversification of academic structures; from the breaking down of those mental barriers which ossified the syllabus and examination system two generations ago. With these changes, of course, have come dangers. The danger of syllabus dilution, the danger of grade inflation, and the danger of relativist academic values. History – as *the* coordinating discipline in the humanities – can resist those dangers. And architectural history will continue to play its part in what will inevitably be a continuing process of debate. Why? Because architectural history operates at several levels: as a register of cultural priorities, as an index of technological change, as a measure of political power, as a barometer of economic movements, and of course as a yardstick of sensibility.

But a Colvinian Inaugural in 1965 might just have captured for Oxford that initiative in architectural history ceded to London in the later-1960s and to

43 Colvin to JMC: 28 Dec. 1981.

44 Crook, 'Architecture and History'; Derek Linstrum 'The Uses of Architectural History Today', in Ben Farmer, Hentie Louw and Adrian Napper, eds., *Companion to Contemporary Architectural Thought* (New York and London, 1993), pp. 227–30.

Cambridge in the later-1970s. As it stands, I fear we have to conclude that the history of architectural history at Oxford has – so far – been a tale of missed opportunities. I leave you with two fragments of anecdotal evidence. In 1849 two important books were published, Edward Freeman's *History of Architecture* and James Fergusson's *Historical Inquiry into the True Principles of Beauty in Art, more especially with reference to Architecture.* Both, in different ways, ground breaking works. Freeman's brief *History* opened up the study of style in building as a narrative of cultural mores and as an explanation of structural expression.[45] Fergusson's *Inquiry* penetrated deeper still into the mysteries of aesthetics: physiological, psychological, ethnological.[46] In the 1970s, the great Arnaldo Momigliano ordered a copy of Freeman's *History* from the Bodleian Library. He found the volume well cared for, but its pages were uncut.[47] In the 1980s a postgraduate pupil of mine ordered a copy of Fergusson's *Inquiry*, again from the Bodleian. He found the book similarly well cared for, but once again its pages were uncut. Well, that was yesterday. Perhaps tomorrow will be a little brighter.

45 A theme considerably developed by Coventry Patmore. See Crook, *The Architect's Secret*, pp. 123, 185.

46 Fergusson cast his net widely. Unless we 'take into account its connexion with ethnography, the *history* of architecture is a mere dry, hard recapitulation of uninteresting facts and terms; but when its relation to the world's history is understood, when we read in their buildings the feelings and aspirations of the people who erected them, and above all through their arts we can trace their relationship to and descent from one another, the study becomes one of the most interesting as well as one of the most useful which can be presented to the inquiring mind' (James Fergusson, *A History of Architecture in All Countries* [London, 1865], intro.).

47 A. D. Momigliano, *Studies in Modern Scholarship*, ed. G. W. Bowersock and J. T. Cornell (Berkeley and Los Angeles, 1994), p. 207.

Index

As his name appears on virtually every page, Howard Colvin has not been separately indexed. Illustrations are referenced by the page number and in italic.